UNDERSTANDING
RON RASH

For Pablo,
From one writer
to another.
Ron Rash
5/16/15

UNDERSTANDING CONTEMPORARY AMERICAN LITERATURE
Matthew J. Bruccoli, Founding Editor
Linda Wagner-Martin, Series Editor

Volumes on

Edward Albee I Sherman Alexie I Nelson Algren I Paul Auster
Nicholson Baker I John Barth I Donald Barthelme I The Beats
Thomas Berger I The Black Mountain Poets I Robert Bly I T. C. Boyle
Truman Capote I Raymond Carver I Michael Chabon I Fred Chappell
Chicano Literature I Contemporary American Drama
Contemporary American Horror Fiction
Contemporary American Literary Theory
Contemporary American Science Fiction, 1926–1970
Contemporary American Science Fiction, 1970–2000
Contemporary Chicana Literature I Robert Coover I Philip K. Dick
James Dickey I E. L. Doctorow I Rita Dove I John Gardner I George Garrett
Tim Gautreaux I John Hawkes I Joseph Heller I Lillian Hellman I Beth Henley
James Leo Herlihy I David Henry Hwang I John Irving I Randall Jarrell
Charles Johnson I Diane Johnson I Adrienne Kennedy I William Kennedy
Jack Kerouac I Jamaica Kincaid I Etheridge Knight I Tony Kushner
Ursula K. Le Guin I Denise Levertov I Bernard Malamud I David Mamet
Bobbie Ann Mason I Colum McCann I Cormac McCarthy I Jill McCorkle
Carson McCullers I W. S. Merwin I Arthur Miller I Stephen Millhauser
Lorrie Moore I Toni Morrison's Fiction I Vladimir Nabokov I Gloria Naylor
Joyce Carol Oates I Tim O'Brien I Flannery O'Connor I Cynthia Ozick
Suzan-Lori Parks I Walker Percy I Katherine Anne Porter I Richard Powers
Reynolds Price I Annie Proulx I Thomas Pynchon I Theodore Roethke
Philip Roth I Richard Russo I May Sarton I Hubert Selby, Jr. I Mary Lee Settle
Sam Shepard I Neil Simon I Isaac Bashevis Singer I Jane Smiley I Gary Snyder
William Stafford I Robert Stone I Anne Tyler I Gerald Vizenor I Kurt Vonnegut
David Foster Wallace I Robert Penn Warren I James Welch I Eudora Welty
Edmund White I Tennessee Williams I August Wilson I Charles Wright

UNDERSTANDING

RON RASH

John Lang

The University of South Carolina Press

© 2014 University of South Carolina

Published by the University of South Carolina Press
Columbia, South Carolina 29208

www.sc.edu/uscpress

Manufactured in the United States of America

23 22 21 20 19 18 17 16 15 14   10 9 8 7 6 5 4 3 2 1

Library of Congress Cataloging-in-Publication Data

Lang, John, 1947–
  Understanding Ron Rash / John Lang.
    pages cm. — (Understanding Contemporary American Literature)
  Includes bibliographical references and index.
  ISBN 978-1-61117-411-3 (hardback) — ISBN 978-1-61117-412-0 (ebook)
  1. Rash, Ron, 1953– —Criticism and interpretation. I. Title.
  PS3568.A698Z73 2014
  813'.54—dc23

                                            2014007288

For Nathan and Lesa, Sarah and Joseph

CONTENTS

SERIES EDITOR'S PREFACE

The Understanding Contemporary American Literature series was founded by the estimable Matthew J. Bruccoli (1931–2008), who envisioned these volumes as guides or companions for students as well as good nonacademic readers, a legacy that will continue as new volumes are developed to fill in gaps among the nearly one hundred series volumes published to date and to embrace a host of new writers only now making their marks on our literature.

As Professor Bruccoli explained in his preface to the volumes he edited, because much influential contemporary literature makes special demands, "the word *understanding* in the titles was chosen deliberately. Many willing readers lack an adequate understanding of how contemporary literature works; that is, of what the author is attempting to express and the means by which it is conveyed." Aimed at fostering this understanding of good literature and good writers, the criticism and analysis in the series provide instruction in how to read certain contemporary writers—explicating their material, language, structures, themes, and perspectives—and facilitate a more profitable experience of the works under discussion.

In the twenty-first century, Bruccoli's prescience gives us an avenue to publish expert critiques of significant contemporary American writing. The series continues to map the literary landscape and to provide both instruction and enjoyment. Future volumes will seek to introduce new voices alongside canonized favorites, to chronicle the changing literature of our times, and to remain, as Bruccoli conceived, contemporary in the best sense of the word.

Linda Wagner-Martin, Series Editor

ACKNOWLEDGMENTS

The initial research for this book was undertaken with the assistance of funding and released time provided by Emory & Henry College through the Henry Carter Stuart Chair in its English Department. I am grateful for that institution's support and encouragement over the twenty-nine years (1983–2012) I taught there. I would also like to thank Jane Caldwell and Patty Greany of the college's Kelly Library for their help in locating elusive materials about Ron Rash and his work. Special thanks to my wife, Esther, whose love and understanding have helped to sustain my academic career for more than forty years, although during the past fifteen months she has wondered aloud more than once, "When is your retirement *really* going to begin?"

My principal indebtedness, however, is to the subject of this study, Ron Rash, whose fiction and poetry have earned my respect and admiration for nearly two decades. During the writing of this monograph, he promptly answered every question I sent to him and insured that I received an advance reading copy of his latest book, *Nothing Gold Can Stay,* well before it was released by HarperCollins. He spent time with me answering additional queries at the 2013 meeting of the Fellowship of Southern Writers, an organization into which he was inducted in 2011. He also agreed to read the final draft of this book's opening chapter to verify the accuracy of its biographical information. It has been a great pleasure to see his publications receive wider and wider acclaim over the past decade, including international recognition. I can only hope that this volume will generate further interest in his achievements as a poet, novelist, and short story writer.

For permission to quote extensively from Rash's poetry, acknowledgment is made to the publishers and individuals listed below:

From *Eureka Mill* by Ron Rash. Copyright © 1998 by Ron Rash. Used by permission of Ron Rash and Hub City Press.

From *Among the Believers* by Ron Rash. Copyright © 2000 by Ron Rash. Used by permission of Ron Rash.

CHAPTER 1

Understanding Ron Rash

In a brief essay, "The Importance of Place," Ron Rash states, "one of the most interesting aspects of literature is how the most intensely regional literature is often the most universal," and he goes on to cite the examples of William Faulkner's Mississippi, Alice Munro's Ontario, Gabriel García Márquez's Colombia, and James Joyce's Dublin.[1] Elsewhere Rash has noted the difference between "regional" and "local color" writing: "Local color is writing that is only about difference—what makes this particular place exotic. Regional writing is writing that shows what is distinct about a place—its language, culture, and all of that—yet at the same time says something universal."[2] Having chosen to ground his work firmly in the history and culture of the American South's Appalachian region, where his ancestors have lived since the mid-1700s, Rash has seen his fiction celebrated not only regionally but also nationally and internationally. *Chemistry and Other Stories* (2007) was a finalist for the PEN/Faulkner Award in 2008, as was his novel *Serena* (2008) in 2009. His fourth collection of short stories, *Burning Bright* (2010), won the prestigious Frank O'Connor International Short Story Award, and his books have been translated into more than a dozen languages, including French, Dutch, Spanish, Japanese, Turkish, and Chinese, evidence that his writing does, indeed, address features of human experience that transcend the local and regional. Responding in the negative when an interviewer asked if he ever consciously thought about being a southern writer, Rash added, "The best of Southern writing has always been universal—the region merely a starting point, not an ending point."[3] Like many other writers from Appalachia and the broader South, Rash is "always wary . . . of adjectives before the word *writer*" because they can easily become terms of disparagement or diminishment, limiting and reductive.[4] Yet the subject matter of his fiction and poetry testifies to his fierce allegiance to Appalachia—its people, its land-scape, its vernacular language, its history, its folklore. Thus Rash's writing has contributed substantially to what Robert Bain and Joseph Flora termed in 1994, the year Rash's first book was published, an Appalachian Renais-sance within the larger Southern Renaissance.[5]

It was Rash's parents and grandparents who instilled in young Ron his sense of identification with the mountain South, specifically Buncombe, Watauga, and Madison Counties in western North Carolina. Although born on September 25, 1953, in Chester, South Carolina, a mill town, and raised in the Appalachian foothills of North Carolina, Rash recalls being aware that "home was always the mountains of North Carolina."[6] His paternal grandparents had moved to Chester from their farm in Buncombe County to work at Eureka Mill. There his mother, Sue, an out-migrant from Watauga County, eventually met his father, James, while both were employed at the mill. James, having dropped out of high school at sixteen, later earned a GED as well as bachelor's and master's degrees, the last from Clemson University. He became professor of art at Gardner-Webb College in Boiling Springs, North Carolina, raising his family there. Yet from age twelve Ron spent summers and many holidays with his maternal grandmother on her farm near Boone in Watauga County, immersing himself in the natural world and in his relatives' storytelling, for "there was no car, . . . no TV," and no air-conditioning.[7] Rash has called the area around his grandmother's farm his "spirit country" and has commented that "that time in the mountains . . . gave me my primary landscape."[8] A slight speech impediment inclined him to listen rather than to talk, so he absorbed family lore as well as Appalachian folklore and regional dialect, material he regularly draws on in his fiction and poetry. In fact he has attributed his becoming a writer to this speech defect.[9]

Among the other influential childhood figures who helped shape Rash's interest in storytelling and writing were his paternal grandfather and his par-ents. In "The Importance of Place" and in several interviews, he has described how his illiterate grandfather led him to believe "words were magical" by recounting different versions of *The Cat in the Hat* each time he "read" that Dr. Seuss book to Ron. Says Rash, "My grandfather could not teach me how to read, but he had taught me how to use my imagination."[10] He also credits his parents with making words magical: "Both were voracious readers, and my mother would take my siblings [a brother and sister] and me to the library every week."[11] His maternal grandmother had been a schoolteacher before marrying, so there were books available at his grandmother's farm, too. His mother earned her college degree in her thirties and then taught elementary school; education was thus highly valued in the Rash household.

As a fifth grader, Rash discovered *The Jesse Stuart Reader,* a book that he read repeatedly over the next few years. Like Rash, Stuart depicts rural Appalachia in assorted genres: novel, short story, and poetry. According to Rash, reading Stuart was "a moment of real revelation for me because suddenly I saw the language that I'd grown up hearing, both in the higher mountains and in the foothills, on the page. And Stuart showed me that there was a beauty to that language, that it was something worthy of literature."[12] A few years later, at age fifteen, Rash read Fyodor Dostoyevsky's *Crime and Punishment* for the first time. "That book made me want to be a writer," he has said.[13] To another interviewer he referred to Dostoyevsky's novel as the book that changed his life: "Until then I had felt that I had entered the book; it was the first book that entered me."[14]

Although he was reading widely in high school and college, Rash has described himself during those years as "mainly an athlete" whose sport was distance running, an activity that he believes provided excellent training for a writer because it taught him discipline and the ability to work alone. "I didn't start writing seriously until my late 20s," he told Robert Birnbaum.[15] By then he had graduated from Gardner-Webb with a B.A. in English and had earned an M.A. from Clemson University. While at Clemson Rash took no creative writing classes, focusing instead on "reading literature." "For me that was good," he has said. "I wasn't really ready to write."[16] After completing his M.A., Rash taught high school for two years in Oconee County, South Carolina, that state's most mountainous county, which provides the setting for his first two novels, *One Foot in Eden* (2002) and *Saints at the River* (2004), and for many of the poems in *Raising the Dead* (2002). He subsequently taught for seventeen years at Tri-County Technical College, a community college in Pendleton, South Carolina, where his typical teaching load was five or six courses per semester, a schedule that would seem to allow little time for his own writing. But Rash was committed to becoming a writer, so he "got up early to write a couple of hours every weekday, wrote weekends and holidays."[17] His writing career received an enormous boost when, starting in 1997, his sister, Kathy, and her husband provided funds over the next three academic years that enabled Rash to purchase release time from some of his courses, an act of generosity and faith in his work that Rash has acknowledged not only by dedicating *Casualties* (2000), his third book, to the couple but also by dedicating his 2012 novel, *The Cove*, to Kathy.

Despite not publishing his first book, *The Night the New Jesus Fell to Earth and Other Stories from Cliffside, North Carolina* (1994), until he was just over forty years old, Rash had been interested in writing even before his college days. Yet as he told interviewer and fellow poet Jeff Daniel Marion,

"I pretty much spent my twenties trying not to write. I wasn't getting any encouragement."[18] In another interview Rash reports, "I didn't write anything good until I was twenty-nine or thirty," though he was "slowly learning [his] craft."[19] By that time he was writing both short stories and poetry, the latter after discovering the work of James Dickey and Seamus Heaney. About the latter he has said that Heaney "described the rural world I'd grown up in, although his was in Northern Ireland." "I suddenly realized," he adds, "that such writing can be universal."[20] This lesson is one Rash found demonstrated as well in the fiction of Flannery O'Connor and Faulkner, who portrayed "a Southern rural world," "the kind of world I came out of," one he recognized on his grandmother's farm and that of an uncle who raised tobacco.[21]

It is amid that rural world that Rash sets much of his writing, an agrarian landscape already diminishing in Appalachia when he was a child but whose disappearance accelerated as the twentieth century proceeded. As Ronald Eller declares, "Between 1950 and 1960, half of the farmers and farm laborers in Appalachia left the land. By the end of the decade, only about 6 percent of the mountain population was employed full time in agriculture." According to Eller, during the 1950s Madison County alone lost some two thousand farms.[22] When Rash was asked by an interviewer about his sense of being "at a crossroads" where an "older culture . . . is going to disappear very quickly" and about the impact of that awareness, Rash responded, "I think it's probably the impetus . . . for [my] writing." He went on to cite the work of Robert Morgan and Wendell Berry as other examples of this desire "to preserve" what is vanishing: "There is a sense that you don't want this to be forgotten, that it had some importance. And I think that's certainly true of Appalachian culture."[23] Combating erasure, combating amnesia—these are major aims of Rash's fiction and poetry, reinforcing the historical impulse so evident not only in his work but also in that of many other writers from Appalachia and the broader South, many of whom have published nonfiction as well: John Ehle, Wilma Dykeman, Harriette Arnow, Mary Lee Settle, Robert Morgan, Robert Penn Warren, and Faulkner. Among the most prominent images of erasure in Rash's books are the flooding of the Jocassee Valley in *One Foot in Eden* and *Raising the Dead,* the Shelton Laurel massacre in *The World Made Straight,* and the clear-cutting of forests in *Serena,* Rash's best-known work. "For whatever reason," Rash told interviewer Jack Shuler, "my imagination seems obsessed with images of loss, things vanishing."[24]

One notable consequence of this "obsession" is Rash's frequent focus on death and the theme of mortality. Likewise his concern for "things vanishing" lends an elegiac tone to much of his work. Yet Rash's effort to forestall erasure, to commemorate Appalachian history and culture, arises not from nostalgia but from his conviction of that culture's ongoing relevance to fundamental human concerns. In a world of increasingly rapid technological and economic changes, what is more universal than a sense of loss? What is more universal than people's shared experience of mortality or of familial bonds? What is more basic—and more urgently in need of recovery—than a recognition of humanity's profound dependence upon the well-being of nature? All these matters are central to Rash's literary vision, one that is simultaneously self-consciously regional and universal. Moreover, as readers of his work quickly realize, Rash carefully avoids sentimentalizing or romanticizing agrarian life.

Because Rash began publishing with smaller regional presses—his first three books were published by the Bench Press, and his next two, both collections of poems, by Iris Press—his work was slow to receive major recognition. Nevertheless over the past twenty years (1994–2013), he has published fourteen books. Asked about his "proudest achievement as a writer," Rash has said, "That I didn't give up, that I had enough faith in myself to keep writing when I was getting rejection slip after rejection slip."[25] Not until his first novel, *One Foot in Eden,* appeared in 2002, winning the Novello Award and receiving high praise from the *Los Angeles Times,* did Rash achieve significant national acclaim, a renown strengthened by the publication of and response to *Chemistry and Other Stories* and *Serena.* Yet ironically, almost two-thirds of the stories in *Chemistry* had appeared seven years before in *Casualties.* Moreover, as early as 1986, eight years before the appearance of his first book, Rash had received an Academy of American Poets Award, followed the next year by a General Electric Foundation Award for Younger Writers. In 1994 he won a fellowship from the National Endowment for the Arts and in 1996 the Sherwood Anderson Prize—all these before the publication of his first collection of poems, *Eureka Mill* (1998). In the years since, amid ongoing recognition at the regional level, he has twice won O. Henry Awards (2005, 2010), for his short stories "Speckled Trout" and "Into the Gorge." Movie versions of *Serena* and *The World Made Straight,* the former starring Jennifer Lawrence and Bradley Cooper, are soon to be released.

Today, as indicated in the opening paragraph of this introduction, Rash has achieved international stature: he has been invited to give readings and to meet with university students in France, Australia, and Ireland, among other countries, and his work is widely reviewed abroad. Nonetheless he maintains his strong tie to the mountain South by serving as Parris Distinguished Professor of Appalachian Cultural Studies at Western Carolina University in Cullowhee, North Carolina. His poetry, short stories, and novels have become major contributions to the Appalachian literary renaissance that began in the 1970s and that continues unabated, but they are also distinguished accomplishments on the national and international literary stage. As Rash told an interviewer in 2006, "I really believe that the best writing coming out of the United States right now is coming from the South. . . . It's amazing how many good writers are working right now, especially in the Southern Appalachians. We can hold our own with any region or sub-region in the U.S."[26] Significantly Rash made this statement before the publication of six of his books, including *Serena* and *Burning Bright,* a novel and short story collection that clearly illustrate his claim.

CHAPTER 2

The Night the New Jesus Fell to Earth, Casualties, and Chemistry

To readers most familiar with Ron Rash the novelist or poet, his extensive work in short fiction over the course of his career may come as a surprise. In fact two of Rash's initial four books, including his first, *The Night the New Jesus Fell to Earth* (1994), and *Casualties* (2000), were collections of stories. Moreover his third such volume, *Chemistry and Other Stories* (2007), a finalist for the PEN/Faulkner Award, reprinted eight selections from *Casualties*—all revised in various ways—among its thirteen stories, a fact that went virtually unnoticed by reviewers of *Chemistry* but one that suggests the high level of Rash's achievement in this genre as early as the late 1990s. It was, after all, the 1986 title story of his first collection that earned Rash the General Electric Younger Writer's Award. About this genre Rash has said, "I just love short stories, and I love to write them. I think short stories are the hardest form to write—harder than poetry and harder than novels. There's a concision such as there is in poetry. . . . Yet at the same time the reader has to feel the satisfaction of a novel, the sense of an arc, a conclusion, a whole experience being rendered."[1]

As a short story writer, Rash generally produces traditional narratives, eschewing the fabulations of magic realism and the self-consciousness of metafiction as well as the vapid style and attenuated characterization of much of literary minimalism. His short fiction is richly detailed both in setting and characterization and presents a wide array of situations and types of people. It is also energized by thematic complexity and nuanced shadings of feeling that engage readers with the moral and emotional challenges his characters confront. Rash's prose style is usually simple and direct, with few of the baroque rhetorical flourishes that mark Faulkner's fiction or that of Cormac McCarthy, despite Rash's admiration for both authors. "I try to write as clean a sentence as I can," he says. "I hope the reader senses a lyricism there but one that is also taut."[2] Stylistically, then, Rash is closer to Ernest Hemingway than to Faulkner, and he relies on dramatic incidents and the emotions inherent in them to insure reader involvement. Another impressive trait of his short stories is their use of widely varied points of view, both first and third person, including an assortment of female as well as male first-person narrators. States Rash, "I like that challenge of entering a sensibility different from my own. I'm really not much interested in writers who limit themselves to a single sensibility. The trait I prize is the one that Keats prized in Shakespeare: negative capability. That, to me, is the greatest literary artistry, where you can be anyone, anything."[3]

While Rash is known for grounding his fiction and poetry in Appalachia, *The Night the New Jesus Fell to Earth and Other Stories from Cliffside, North Carolina* is set in a small piedmont community with only one stop-light, a town dominated economically by a cotton mill but also home to a junior college. Cliffside (an actual town of that name is located a few miles from Boiling Springs) thus combines features of the author's birthplace in Chester, South Carolina, with those of the town in which he grew up. The name Cliffside suggests the precariousness of the town's situation, its liability to topple or slip, a trait consistent with Rash's conception of human nature and with the theological observation made by Tracy, one of the book's three first-person narrators, that "it's a fallen world," a phrase repeated twice more in the volume's title story.[4] A cliff, of course, is also an apt place from which to make a Kierkegaardian leap of faith, and as the collection's title indicates, religious concerns are an important subject for Rash, here and throughout his career.

But equally important is a more general experience of change and loss, evident in the book's brief italicized opening section, which reports the de-struction by fire of Greene's Café, now "nothing but smoke and ashes" (1). The burning of this restaurant, a business mentioned more than a dozen times in the ten stories that compose the book, comes to represent the increasing erosion of small-town communities and their way of life. Also vanishing or marginalized is the agrarian landscape that surrounds Cliffside, although Randy Ledbetter, another of the three narrators, has recently bought and moved to a chicken farm after earlier selling his family's farm to please a wife who subsequently divorces him. The third narrator, Vincent Hampton, has an uncle who farms, though Vincent himself lives in Cliffside. On several occasions Rash refers to the "New South" and its impact on towns such as Cliffside.

Unlike any of Rash's other story collections, this first book is structured as a cycle of interrelated stories somewhat in the manner of Sherwood Anderson's *Winesburg, Ohio*. Instead of a single central character like Anderson's George Willard, whose experiences are described from third-person point of view, Rash portrays three first-person narrators and thus draws more directly on oral storytelling traditions. On the night of the fire, Tracy, Randy, and Vincent gather at Randy's farm and presumably share the stories that appear in the subsequent pages, following the italicized prologue narrated by Tracy, who likewise narrates the book's brief epilogue. The stories themselves are divided into three numbered sections of three, four, and three stories each, a structure that enables Rash to highlight Vincent, who tells not only the first and last stories but also the opening and closing stories of part 2.

Although Rash has said that his fiction is "not consciously" autobiographical, Vincent shares several key traits with his creator, whose middle name is Vincent.[5] His father is an art professor named James; his father grew up in a mill village and worked at the mill, where Vincent's grandfather was also employed; Vincent is a cross-country distance runner, as Rash was in high school and college; and Vincent's eccentric father had proposed naming him Hieronymus Michelangelo (130), as Rash's father had wanted to name him Rembrandt.[6] In the book's opening story, Vincent even refers to the college's biology teacher as Dr. Brown, a nod to Rash's friendship with Dr. Les Brown, professor of biology at Gardner-Webb, whose wife, Joyce, a professor of English, encouraged Rash to write and has championed his work in essays, reviews, and an interview. Moreover in the book's present time, Vincent has temporarily returned to Cliffside to visit his mother, his father having died, as Rash's did when the author was just twenty-five. Yet except in the book's opening story, "Badeye," Vincent's narratives deal as much or more with his father or with other residents of Cliffside as they do with himself.

The title "Badeye," though it nominally refers to a bootlegger named Carter whose wife had stabbed him in his right eye with an ice pick some ten years earlier, also addresses the issue of poor judgment, of faulty vision beyond mere physical eyesight, for the story can be read as a retelling of the biblical account of the Fall—minus, significantly, the figure of Eve as tempter. Rash's use of violence and the comic grotesque in this story is reminiscent of O'Connor, one of his major influences.[7] Badeye, who also sells snow cones to Cliffside's children, has a "serpent [a king cobra] tattooed on his shoulder," and he thus intrigues eight-year-old Vincent, whose "obsession with snakes" both Badeye and Vincent's father foster, though Vincent's mother is terrified of them and sees her son's interest in them as "further proof . . . of man's fallen nature" (7, 14). By summer's end the boy has thirty-three cages filled with these reptiles on his family's carport, among them a venomous coral snake provided by Badeye on the condition that Vincent deliver a mason jar of moonshine to one of Badeye's customers. This assignment the boy completes—but only after sampling the jar's contents. Upon returning home Vincent reaches into the coral snake's cage and is bitten, his scream— "not one of pain but of knowledge"—alerting his parents (25). Although Badeye is obviously a tempter figure, Rash makes clear that Vincent's father abets his son's fascination with snakes, borrowing cages from the college's biologist and giving his son for Christmas "a massive tome big as our family Bible . . . titled *Snakes of the World*" (15). The men of Cliffside, readers are also told, tend to view Badeye more as a scapegoat than a tempter, for, cognizant of their own flaws as husbands, they believe "Badeye's right eye had died for all their sins" (9). While such a statement is tinged with comic irony, this opening story reinforces the moral and religious concerns evident in the collection's title and underscored by Rash's placement of the title story immediately after "Badeye."

The other three stories narrated by Vincent—"Yard of the Month," "Notes from Beyond the Pale," and "My Father's Cadillacs"—show the boy steadily growing older. He is twelve in the first of these, fourteen in the second, and passes from fifteen to eighteen in the last, a chronological progression that reflects his emotional and mental maturation. "Yard of the Month" focuses primarily on Vincent's father, while "Notes" feature's Vincent's account of a resident of Cliffside who returns from his college years at Harvard with a Yankee wife, who then criticizes the town's residents, including her husband, Homer, a high school history teacher, for their provinciality. Eventually Emily leaves her husband and returns north, one of several characters in the book who reflect the impact of outsiders in the New South.

The most important and accomplished of these three stories is "My Father's Cadillacs" because in it Rash underscores issues of social class and class differences that recur throughout his career, not only in his fiction but also in his poetry, most notably in *Eureka Mill*. Rash skillfully avoids didacticism by leavening these concerns with a strong admixture of humor, comedy that turns on Vincent's father's tendency to purchase his Cadillacs, much to his son's dismay, from undertakers, leaving his son no option but to drive his date to the senior prom in a vehicle that appears to be leading a funeral procession and that induces oncoming cars to pull off the road and stop, in traditional southern fashion, out of respect for the (presumed) deceased (137–38). Yet despite the profound embarrassment occasioned by such an event, Vincent comes to recognize and appreciate his father's motive for buying a Cadillac: "Because owning a Cadillac shows exactly how far

I've come from that mill village where I grew up," his father remarks (133). James also takes his son past homes in nearby Shelby "five times the size of [Vincent's] grandmother's home a half-mile away," pointing out "the largest of the houses," the one in which Old Man Calhoun, the mill's owner, had lived when James and Vincent's grandfather worked there (136). The closing paragraphs of this story, the final one in the collection, record Vincent's reflections about his grandfather and father, emphasizing their aspirations: "I thought of my grandfather, working most of his life in the card room of the cotton mill, breathing the cotton dust that eventually killed him, dreaming of a son who would never have to see the inside of a cotton mill, but never living long enough to see his dream come true, to see his son, my father teaching at a college. . . . My father, too, dreaming of a life beyond the mill village" (141). That Vincent identifies with his father's stance is evident in his own purchase of a 1978 Cadillac driven in the years following his father's death, the car's date of manufacture being the year of Rash's father's death.

By setting this story's final scene in spring, with dogwoods in bloom, Rash inserts a note of optimism, for as Vincent's grandmother observes, "there is something about a dogwood in the spring that fills a body with hope. It makes you feel like all your dreams can still come true" (141). Vincent, too, sees the "blossoms blazing, bright as dreams against the darkness," in the story's final phrase. But part of the darker side of human experience portrayed by Rash resides in the economic disparities and social injustice that plague American society. As Rash told an interviewer, "I was always aware of class distinctions and particularly of the feudal system that operated in the mills, of that hierarchy and the places that people were supposed to occupy in it, that structure of complete control. . . . My class awareness, and sometimes class resentment, came out of my family's personal experience."[8]

Although Vincent is the narrator accorded the largest number of stories, Rash gives almost equal prominence to Tracy, who narrates the book's opening and closing italicized sections and three stories, including the title story, with explicitly religious subject matter. Tracy is the first of many female protagonists in Rash's fiction, a carpenter by trade and thus a figure who subverts women's traditional roles. For more than five years, Tracy has been divorced from her former husband, Larry Rudisell—a used-car dealer and the "new Jesus" of the title story—whom she labels "a snake" in that story's opening paragraph (29). Intelligent, resilient, hard-working, and deeply religious, Tracy represents the best of the Southern Baptist denomination in which Rash was raised. Tracy also narrates the most humorous stories in this collection: not only the title story but also "Raising the Dead" and "Judgment Day," all of which contain comic hyperbole in the tall tale tradition.

The satirical title story turns on humor of character and action. Larry, motivated by greed and self-interest, having had what he calls a "vision," proposes that Cliffside Baptist Church mount a Good Friday reenactment of the Crucifixion, with Larry in the role of Jesus. Though controversy ensues, Larry's proposal ultimately gains congregational approval, with Tracy asked by the new preacher to complete the carpentry work required. But when Tracy arrives at the church with eight-inch-thick poles for the crosses, poles she knows will make stable supports, Larry rejects them, insisting that "they looked like telephone poles, that he was supposed to be Jesus, not the Wichita Lineman" (36). As Eudora Welty does in "Why I Live at the P.O.," Rash incorporates other such popular culture references to gauge the quality of Larry's mind and his distortion of authentic piety—as when he appears at the church "pointing and waving his arm like he was a Hollywood director" (35). Larry's ulterior motive is revealed on Good Friday when he sets up at the church a portable electric sign that reads, "The Crucifixion Of JESUS CHRIST Is Paid for and Presented by LARRY RUDISELL's Used Cars Of Cliffside, North Carolina. . . . If JESUS Had Driven A Car, He Would Have Bought It At LARRY's," the capitalization of their names indicating Larry's equation of himself with Jesus (39). Rash provides a hilarious account of the chaos that ensues when it becomes clear that the flimsy crosses Larry has had installed will not bear his weight or that of the two thieves beside him. Satire, multiple ironies, and slapstick comedy combine to make this story one of Rash's funniest. The broken jaw and nose Larry incurs when his cross collapses are ironically apt, for both are parts of the body associated with lying (as in the story of Pinocchio in the case of the nose), a sin that confirms Tracy's assumption—and Rash's—that "we live in a fallen world" (43). Yet as Tracy adds in the story's final sentence, "even in a fallen world things can sometimes look up" (43).

"Raising the Dead" is a less accomplished story, but one that illustrates Rash's interest in conflicts involving both social class and race. The story turns on Mrs. Calhoun's decision, not for the first time, to transfer her church membership and to exhume her husband's body for reburial in her new church's cemetery. Because Mrs. Calhoun owns, as her husband had before her, "the biggest cotton mill in Cleveland County" (65), home to Cliffside and Shelby (and Boiling Springs), few people are inclined to oppose her wishes—even when those wishes extend, in tall-tale fashion, to her insistence that her deceased husband, Pappy, be numbered among the church's voting members and that she be allowed to cast his vote: "the deacons said it qualified as an absentee ballot" (66). In this instance, however, Mrs. Calhoun's desire to change churches arises not from doctrinal disputes but from Cliffside Baptist's having allowed an African missionary, "a negro," to speak to the congregation (67). In addition to opposing Mrs. Calhoun's racism, Tracy and Jessie, the local undertaker who has asked Tracy to make a coffin for the pauper Dooley Ross, want to see Dooley treated decently in death. Class resentment plays a significant role in their decision to switch the corpses' coffins, because Jessie's parents had worked at Calhoun Mill and Pappy had fired Tracy's uncle. As a result of their actions, Pappy is placed in the simple coffin Tracy has built and is interred, ironically, in an African American church's graveyard, the only plot inexpensive enough for Dooley's benefactors to purchase. Meanwhile Dooley lies in Pappy's ornate coffin, which continues to migrate regularly to new cemeteries at Mrs. Calhoun's ecclesiastical whims. Like several of the chapters in Fred Chappell's *I Am One of You Forever,* this story details a *rusty,* an Appalachian term for a practical joke. In doing so it treats comically what becomes a major motif in Rash's subsequent poetry and fiction: raising the dead, the title of his third volume of poems, a motif that not only embraces orthodox Christian belief in the resurrection but also affirms the resurrection power of memory and of the literary imagination.

Tracy's third story, "Judgment Day," also features her ex-husband, Larry, and other members of the congregation at Cliffside Baptist, who resort to public confessions of sin one Sunday when record-setting rains flood the church cemetery, causing coffins to rise from graves, and when a car horn's bleating of Elvis Presley's "Heartbreak Hotel" following an accident near the church leads the congregation to believe they are hearing the angel Gabriel announce the Last Judgment. In the comic chaos that ensues, Larry's fiancée, Wanda, announces that she's been unfaithful to him, and Larry himself feels compelled to acknowledge that he has "put sawdust in gear boxes and rolled back odometers" (123). Though primarily a comic tale, this story also highlights the moral and religious thrust of Rash's work by emphasizing accountability for one's actions even as it pokes fun at the hyperactive consciences of some members of the congregation. Amid the plot's comic confusions, Tracy discerns what she calls "a true act of God," and the story closes with her gesture of kindness toward the abandoned Wanda, conduct that seems to Tracy "the Christian thing to do" (116, 125). Larry, however, is too completely a villain to produce the moral complexity Rash creates in his best fiction.

Of the book's three narrators, Randy is the least well developed, his conflict with his wife, Darlene (who in Randy's first story intends to divorce him and later does, remarrying soon after), providing the narrative thread that links his three tales, "Love and Pain," "Between the States," and the intensely humorous "Redfish, Possums, and the New South." Unlike the past-tense stories of Vincent and Tracy, Randy's are told in present tense, thereby lending immediacy to the crises he faces. Imagery of blindness ties Randy's first two stories to the book's opening story, "Badeye": "Love and Pain" finds him "wishing I had a pair of blinders like they put on mules" to resist the appeal of Darlene's beauty (44), and "Between the States" depicts Randy (who is imbibing moonshine at his high school reunion) recalling moonshine's reputation for blinding its drinkers (76). Less educated than Vincent, Randy allows Rash to demonstrate his skill with regional dialect and vernacular speech, as when Randy refers to his prospective business partner, Gerald, as "half bubble off plumb" and later tells him, "Your mind is so open that peanut you call a brain has done fallen out" (100).

Readers familiar with Rash's first novel, *One Foot in Eden*, will note some significant similarities between events in that novel and Randy's situation. For example, as in the marriage of Amy and Billy Holcomb, so in Randy's marriage Darlene's principal reason for seeking to divorce him is his inability to give her a child; and just as Sheriff Alexander and his wife struggle over social class differences, so do Darlene and Randy, who tells Darlene, "I tried not to act like a redneck," only to hear her reply, "And failed" (48). Yet readers are not given a sufficiently detailed account of this couple's past to sympathize fully with Randy's plight, especially not when he flees the reunion and momentarily considers suicide while standing on the Broad River Bridge that joins North Carolina to South Carolina (83). Nevertheless this image of liminality is one to which Rash returns in subsequent poems, stories, and novels, including *Saints at the River* (2004). Ultimately rejecting suicide, Randy concludes "Between the States" hoping for renewal, a recovery he seems to achieve when he likewise rejects Gerald's ludicrous scheme to raise possums as a culinary delicacy for sale to New York restaurants and instead buys the former Caldwell chicken farm, even though he recognizes that "nobody seems to be farming in the New South" (99).

Rash ends his first book with Tracy "watch[ing] Cliffside disappear in the rearview mirror" of her truck (143). As Rash has said of this volume, "I had to write first about the foothills so that I could move my writing into the world that was ultimately my subject matter"—the world of the Appalachian Mountains in western North Carolina.[9] Nevertheless Rash's second book of stories, *Casualties*, contains at least five stories set explicitly in Cliffside or in Cleveland County even as it shifts the major locus of his fiction to Watauga County. Despite Rash's seemingly deprecating comments about *The Night the New Jesus Fell to Earth*, the book is more than apprentice fiction, for as Gilbert Allen wrote of the volume in the *Georgia Review*, "Rash . . . creates memorable voices and a host of unforgettable images" in this "substantial contribution to recent Southern fiction."[10] The collection also introduces several of the subjects and concerns that Rash developed more fully in later books: the power of storytelling in grappling with change and loss; the nature and roles of religious belief; family conflicts and failures of love; and social class differences and issues of economic justice. Perhaps most important, this first book deserves to be read for its author's exuberant sense of humor, an attribute that became less notable as Rash turned to the grimmer characters and events of *Casualties* and of many of his other subsequent publications.

More widely reviewed than his first book of stories, though largely in regional journals and newspapers, *Casualties* comprises fourteen stories, seven of them previously published in such periodicals as *Shenandoah,* the *Greensboro Review,* and the *South Carolina Review.* As the book's title indicates, many of the characters are wounded, whether physically or emotionally. While warfare and the violence of combat are one recurring source of such injuries in Rash's fiction, the majority of these stories deal with less tangible peacetime wounds and woes. Says Rash, "To me, what's interesting is how someone in life responds to these wounds. . . . All people have their wounds."[11] His outlook here reveals one important basis for his assumption that the universal can be conveyed through a focus on the regional, as was discussed in the opening chapter of this book. The cover art of *Casualties* consists of a sketch made by Rash's father,[12] a fitting detail for a volume that includes "Chemistry," a story in which Rash has said he consciously explored his relationship with his father.[13]

Initial reviews of the collection were quite positive, with one reviewer referring to it as a "book of insistently quiet significance" and another praising it as "unforgettable, . . . a perfect balance of imagination and craft."[14] Yet a third concluded his review as follows: "Southern Appalachian fiction for the last 20 or so years has been in its heyday. With this solid collection, Ron Rash joins the ranks of its best practitioners."[15] These reviewers were particularly impressed by the stories "Last Rite," "Chemistry," "The Projectionist's Wife," "Overtime," and "Return," and they noted the book's diversity of characters and situations, features, like its greater depth of characterization and its careful control of varied narrative points of view, that mark a major advance over Rash's first book. Whereas that initial collection utilized just three first-person narrators, *Casualties* has ten, along with four stories told from a skillfully delimited third-person point of view.

Rash opens the book with such a third-person account, "Last Rite," based on a Rash family story about a mother's quest to determine the state, North Carolina or Tennessee, in which her murdered son was killed and buried, information she wants to record in the family Bible. (A poem of this

title appeared in the same year in *Among the Believers*.) Set near Boone,
North Carolina, in the post-Civil War era, this narrative loosely links Rash's
first two books of stories by having the murdered son and his mother bear
the same surname, Hampton, as does Vincent of *New Jesus*. Such connections reappear elsewhere in this collection—and throughout Rash's fiction
and poetry—as he builds up and revisits an interlinked, vividly imagined
fictional world, much as Faulkner did with his Yoknapatawpha County. In
"Last Rite" Sarah Hampton, whose grief is movingly portrayed, hires and ac-
companies a surveyor who identifies the location of Elijah's grave as Watauga
County, North Carolina. As in much of Rash's work, the emotions displayed
in this story are understated, with Sarah a study in stoicism but also a figure
of deep familial love. Her quest for closure is a quest for knowledge—and
for the consolation, often short-lived, that knowledge brings.

"Chemistry," the book's second story, is among its finest, tied geographi-
cally both to Cliffside and to Watauga County, where the narrator's father,
another Hampton, had grown up. Here Rash returns to the religious concerns so prevalent in his first collection, though he deals with them in a far
more nuanced manner. The story's seventeen-year-old narrator, Joel, seems
a version of the earlier book's Vincent, although Joel's father, Paul, is a high
school chemistry teacher, not an art professor, who has had a mental breakdown and undergone electroshock therapy. Upon his release from the hospital, Paul refuses to take the medicine his doctor has prescribed and instead
seeks psychological equilibrium by leaving Cliffside Presbyterian Church and
"driving up to Cleveland County's mountainous northern corner to attend
a Pentecostal church" like the one of his childhood and youth in Watauga
County, his conversion to Presbyterianism after his marriage having "sig-
naled a social as well as religious transformation, a sign of upward mobility
from hardscrabble Appalachian beginnings."[16] In one respect, however, Paul
does heed his doctor's advice: he takes up scuba diving as a hobby—a hobby,
any hobby, having been recommended by the doctor "to keep his [Paul's]
mind off his mind" (14 [24]). For a time Paul enlists Joel in this activity,
though Joel soon abandons it in what seems an act of self-willed blindness,
his "growing certainty that many things in the world were better left hidden"
(19 [29]). Rather than joining his father in South Mountain Reservoir, Joel
watches him descend into the lake "toward mysteries I no longer wished to
fathom" (20 [29]).

By story's end Paul has died on one of his dives due to "nitrogen narcosis,
sometimes called rapture of the deep" (28 [38]). But before then Joel has
followed his father to a Pentecostal service of healing at which Joel hears
speaking in tongues and sees the church's pastor handling a rattlesnake

before he abruptly departs, unwilling to see more. When Joel admits to his father that he does not understand what draws Paul to this church, Paul tries to explain that his doctor's diagnosis of "a chemical imbalance" as the source of his depression is simplistic. Like his pastor, who had caused his wife's and daughter's deaths in a car wreck, Paul finds that "there was nothing in this world to sustain him, so he had to look somewhere else" (26 [36]). As Joel reflects on his father's death, recalling the coroner's discovery that Paul had removed his diving mask just before drowning, an action the coroner views as the result of irrational impulse, he considers another possibility: that his father's gesture arose from "a reaction to something realized," from his sense of being "astonished at what he drifted toward" (29 [cf.39]).

In this story Rash subtly addresses the tension between science and religion, matter and spirit, head and heart, major motifs not only of American literature at least since Nathaniel Hawthorne but also of Western philosophy. As Paul tells Joel, "Sometimes you have to search for [solutions] in places where only the heart can go" (26 [36]), a claim through which Rash alludes to Blaise Pascal's famous statement "The heart has its reasons, which reason does not know."[17] Significantly, in Welsh folklore, which Rash often incorporates into his work, water is a conduit to the spiritual realm and thus an apt emblem of the unfathomable.[18] The mysteries Joel associates with the depths of the reservoir are reminiscent of the sense of mystery that Rash himself developed on his grandmother's farm in Watauga County. "The world is a very mysterious place," he has said. "The mountains taught me that. And that's a great gift for a writer, for a poet, to sense the mystery."[19] According to Rash, one of the principal functions of storytelling is "to deepen the mystery"—a phrase he attributes to Francis Bacon—"to deepen the wonder of simply being alive."[20] Asked by an interviewer whether he is a religious person, Rash replied, "Yes, and I come out of a religious culture," although, he added, "that doesn't mean that I haven't gone through periods of skepticism."[21]

The names Rash assigns to the father and son in this story, like the biblical names of the mother and son in "Last Rite," are meant to suggest the pervasive influence of Appalachian religious culture, but those names also assume added significance, combining as they do an Old Testament prophet and the Jewish convert to Christianity who authored much of the New Testament. In Hebrew the name Joel means "the Lord is God," and Joel was a prophet who, though he warned of imminent judgment and destruction, also spoke of God as "gracious and merciful, slow to anger, and abounding in steadfast love" (Joel 2:13 [RSV]). Of equal significance, the father's removal of his diving mask in "Chemistry" is an act that seems to allude to St. Paul's first letter to the Corinthians, in which he writes, "Now we see as through a glass, darkly, but then shall we see Him [Christ] face to face" (13:12). It is also St. Paul who speaks of "having the eyes of your hearts enlightened" (Ephesians 1:18), an image consistent with Rash's emphasis in "Chemistry" on the heart as a counterweight to the mind. As Peter Makuck states about this story's closing, which he calls "a convincing stunner," it "suggests our little lives are not so much rounded by a blank sleep, but by an astonishing dimension we wake to at last."[22] Just as Sarah in "Last Rite" thinks the mounded earth of Elijah's grave looks "like it's pregnant" (11 [49]), so in "Chemistry" Rash has Joel hint at life beyond the experience of death, as Rash himself does in many of his poems and in his 2013 short story "Something Rich and Strange."

Of the three other stories in part 1 of *Casualties*—"The Way Things Are," "The Projectionist's Wife," and "Cold Harbor"—the strongest is "Cold Harbor," which returns to the physical setting and third-person point of view of "Last Rite." In this case the protagonist, Anna, is not a resident of Watauga County, however, but a visitor from Washington, D.C., a nurse during the Korean War who arrives in North Carolina to see what has become of a severely wounded soldier whose life she saved two years earlier. Rash also links this story to "Last Rite" by giving the soldier the surname Triplett, the name of the young man to whom Sarah's widowed daughter-in-law is engaged. The story's title not only foreshadows the disappointment Anna will encounter but also alludes to one of the bloodiest battles of the Civil War, one in which, Rash writes, "Grant had lost seven thousand men in eight minutes" (49 [98]). Set in the 1950s, this story evokes a history of national and international warfare, as opposed to the personal violence threatened or committed in "The Projectionist's Wife."

The maimed soldier, Josh Triplett, lost an arm and incurred a serious neck wound that resulted in a laryngectomy, requiring him to speak through a stoma in his throat and distorting his speech. Josh is the first of several characters in Rash's fiction to have lost a hand or arm, anticipating the Confederate officer in the poem "The Dowry," Galloway in *Serena*, and Hank Shelton in *The Cove*. But Josh's physical injuries find a parallel in Anna's psychological wounds, which have left her deeply depressed and led to the dissolution of her marriage. Neither Josh nor Anna seems open to the future in this story set in the past: Josh is an embittered, unwilling survivor, and Anna, returning to Washington at story's end, anticipates another night when she will "[lie] down again with the dead" who haunt her (55 [105]). In an era before the term was coined, she clearly struggles with posttraumatic stress disorder, and she thus enables Rash to emphasize the anguish of more recent veterans of combat, soldiers and civilians alike. References to the heart help to unify this narrative, as when Anna, approaching the trailer in which Josh is living,

encounters "a scarecrow dressed in a helmet and camouflage, . . . a Purple
Heart pinned at the center of the empty chest" (51 [101]) and when Josh's
mother explains to her, in words as applicable to Anna as to Josh, "Some
grief is like barbed wire that's been wrapped around a tree. . . . The longer
it's there the deeper the barbs go, the closer to the tree's heart" (54–55 [104]).

The power of Rash's closing image in "Cold Harbor," of Anna's lying
down again with the dead, is matched by the arresting opening sentences in
several of the stories in part 2. "Not Waving but Drowning," for example,
begins "Across the room a woman cups her front teeth in the palm of her
left hand" (74 [cf. 73]), while "Honesty" opens with the statement "I met
LeAnn McIntyre on a date suggested by my wife" (95 [107]). The five first-
person narrators of the stories in part 2 are quite diverse: among them the
lover—and target—of the knife thrower in a carnival, a husband whose wife
is having her third miscarriage, and a college professor. Yet the title of the
story about the knife thrower, "Dangerous Love," could be applied to four
of the stories in this section, "Summer Work" being the lone exception. The
vulnerability inherent in love, in emotional commitments to another person,
is among Rash's major themes, one apparent also in "Last Rite" as well as
in "Time Zones" and "Casualties and Survivors" in part 3. While two of the
stories in part 2 involve characters living in Cliffside and one takes place in
an unnamed university town, the other two are set in upstate South Carolina,
an area Rash continued to explore in the poems of *Raising the Dead* and in
his first two novels. In all these stories, Rash makes effective use of flashbacks
and memories, thus underscoring his belief in the significance of the past,
whether as shaping force, as negative example, or as resource in the present.

Among the great strengths of these stories is Rash's ability to generate
sympathy for his characters and their plights. In "Not Waving but Drowning," for instance, the Tripletts, Mary and her unnamed husband, who
narrates this present-tense story, wait in a hospital emergency room to
learn whether her pregnancy has ended in another miscarriage. A flashback
describes the picnic at Lake Jocassee during which the couple made love,
Mary telling her husband, "I want us to try again" despite two previous
miscarriages (81 [80]). Earlier that day the couple had boated on the lake,
beneath which lie farmhouses, barns, and other buildings inundated when
Duke Power Company flooded the valley. Staring down into the reservoir's
depths, Mary remarks, "It's like if you watched long enough somebody
would walk out of one of those houses and look up and wave at us" (79
[79]), an image Rash repeats in *Raising the Dead* and *One Foot in Eden*. At
story's end, then, the reader knows the news the husband is about to hear
will not be good when he comments, as he heads off to meet the doctor, "I

walk slow as the dead might walk across the cold and silent floor of Lake Jocassee" (82 [82]). Adding to the irony of this couple's circumstances is the contrast between their genuine love for one another and the presence in the waiting room of a wife who clutches the front teeth her husband has knocked out. The story's title comes from Stevie Smith's 1957 poem of the same title, a poem in which the speaker states, "it was too cold always," not just on the occasion of his drowning: "I was much too far out all my life / And not waving but drowning."[23] These lines reinforce the narrator's sense of the risk he and Mary have taken with her third pregnancy, for he realizes that "our future together would come down to this last gamble," a bet they appear to have lost, becoming casualties once more (81 [80]).

In the final story in part 2, "My Father Like a River," Rash again uses the water imagery so prominent in this collection and, indeed, throughout his work. The river of this title is the Heraclitean river of flux, of change—in this case one involving the unnamed narrator's father's loss of his supervisory position at Hamrick's mill, a position he held for just two years before a change in the mill's leadership results in his firing. While the previous owner had valued the father's many years of "hard work and experience" in the mill's weave room, his son-in-law rejects Mr. Hamrick's viewpoint after the older man's death. "He was thirty-five years old, a man with a wife, four children, and no job," says the narrator of his father (107). In this story Rash writes movingly of the vicissitudes of the working class and of the family's loss of their suburban home, "the first home in three generations someone in my father's family had owned" (108). But the narrator also focuses on his father's saving a younger son from drowning on the New River in Watauga County in the same November that he lost his position in "the white-collar world"; during the rescue he loses his wallet and the week's pay it contains (107). The narrator, fourteen years old at the time, thinks of the New River as "moving in the wrong direction" because it flows north, not south, "as though the river had found a way to defy the law of gravity" (107, 111). Such defiance also characterizes the father, who saves a child whose own conduct has put himself and his family at risk. The father eventually finds a job back in another mill's weave room, the place "where he had started out at eighteen"; yet, as the narrator adds, "though he would work at Shuford Mill for thirty years, he'd never wear a tie [again] or make half the salary he'd brought home those two years he was a manager" (114). Rather than seeing him as a failure, however, the narrator chooses to remember how his father "found something worth holding on to in that wrong-flowing current that carried all of our lives" (114). Behind this story lies the shadow of both Robert Frost's poem "West-Running Brook," with its image of a white wave that "runs counter to itself,"[24] and the parable of the Prodigal Son. As in that parable, the father's action is a measure of his love; the "something worth holding on to" he has found is his family, one of the principal sources of meaning and value not just in Appalachia but across the globe.

Family ties are also a prominent feature of three of the four stories in the final section of *Casualties:* "Time Zones," "Casualties and Survivors," and "Return." The first of these is the slightest, though Rash later mined it for background details about Leonard Shuler in *The World Made Straight.* The second, the book's penultimate story, revisits the heart imagery so important in "Chemistry" and "Cold Harbor." This third-person narrative, told from a woman's point of view, opens in the Cleveland County Library, where Rachel is checking out two library books, one, recommended by her husband Allen's cardiologist, on heart attacks and one on sign language because, as she tells Allen, "I just thought it would be interesting to try and learn something new" (141). Rash's choice of present tense in this story reflects Rachel's desire to help Allen begin anew after his recent heart attack, for she has noticed that he is not "his old self" (142): "It is as if he were a ghost still burdened by a body" (143). Yet as Rachel had earlier observed, looking at other patients in the coronary care unit, their bodies were "the very equipment that keeps them alive" (138). In the lovemaking Rachel initiates in the story's closing scene, she helps transform Allen from casualty to survivor. "They lay their hands upon each other's bodies and speak love's old, final language," Rash writes, signaling that this couple's marriage of twenty-five years will survive Allen's medical crisis (145).

The book's concluding story, "Return," extends the optimism evident in the preceding story while helping to unify the book as a whole by recurring to the settings and surnames of "Last Rite." Although the events in "Return" are based on the experiences of Rash's uncle, Robert Holder, a veteran of World War II, this story names the soldier Hampton and situates his home in Watauga County. In fact this Hampton ascends snowy Dismal Mountain, at the foot of which Elijah Hampton of "Last Rite" had built a house for himself and his bride, a place that gives Dismal Gorge its name in Rash's poetry. Rash also links "Return" to "Cold Harbor" by referring to Lawson Triplett, the father of the maimed soldier in the earlier tale. Skillfully interweaving present-tense scenes of Hampton's trek home with the soldier's memories of combat in the Pacific—events also recounted in the poems "Return" and "In the Solomons" in *Among the Believers*—Rash counterpoints the winter landscape through which Hampton travels with the springtime he antici-pates, with its promise of renewal. Having survived, thanks to his helmet, a Japanese sniper's attack, Hampton drinks from that helmet at the family's spring in the story's closing scene, another instance of Rash's pervasive water imagery, in this case of water not as destructive but as life enhancing. Yet as he passes the cemetery at his family's church, Hampton momentarily feels that the new gravestone he sees there "is his own, that he's really still in the Philippines, dreaming this, maybe even dying or dead" (150), words reminiscent of the plot of Ambrose Bierce's famous "Occurrence at Owl Creek Bridge," an allusion that relates the violence of World War II to that of the Civil War, as "Cold Harbor" links the Korean War to that earlier conflict. Warfare remains one of the major subjects of Rash's fiction, and *Casualties* is his first book to make that concern apparent.

Although the term *casualties* can refer to victims of accidents or of circumstances beyond the individual's control (such as the job loss experienced in "My Father Like a River" or the mental breakdown in "Chemistry"), Rash's stories often turn on choices people consciously make and for which they become accountable. In "Casualties and Survivors," Rachel thinks of her children's "essential decency confirmed in small, quiet acts of consideration and generosity" (141). But Mrs. Merwin of "The Projectionist's Wife," Clifford of "Summer Work," the husband and wife of "Honesty," and Cedric of "Overtime" all make destructive choices, decisions that harm themselves or others. As Rash's literary career progressed, he came to focus increasingly on such issues of moral choice, avoiding heavy-handed didacticism yet infusing his stories and novels with a sense of urgency that American society heighten its awareness of the devastation wrought by such phenomena as the drug epidemic in Appalachia and elsewhere and by assaults on the environment, as well as by economic injustice, what Edith Wharton termed "the hard considerations of the poor," as Rash quotes her in "Honesty" (98 [111]). *The World Made Straight* and *Serena* both address such matters, and Rash's third book of stories, *Chemistry and Other Stories,* contains material that appears in those novels.

To the eight selections that *Chemistry* reprints from *Casualties,* with varying degrees of revision, Rash added five new works of short fiction, two of which, "Speckled Trout" and "Pemberton's Bride," were incorporated into the two novels mentioned above. In fact *The World Made Straight* had already been published by the time *Chemistry* appeared in print, and the passages that compose "Pemberton's Bride" had been excerpted from a manuscript for *Serena.*[25] Two of these five previously uncollected texts, "Speckled Trout" and "Deep Gap," deal with drug abuse in the mountain South, while "Pemberton's Bride," set in the 1930s, depicts the environmental degradation effected by the timber industry in western North Carolina. The collection's initial story, "Their Ancient, Glittering Eyes," touches on both reverence for nature and, like the book's title story, the nature of reverence, on respect for mystery and wonder as the foundations of religious belief. The fifth new story, "Blackberries in June," uses this regional expression suggestive of marvelous good fortune that verges on the miraculous to meditate on the roles of chance and choice, luck and hard work, in shaping people's lives. As in "My Father Like a River" and the poems of *Eureka Mill,* here Rash adopts the working-class perspective that continues to be a prominent dimension of his work.

Like Rash's first two collections of stories, *Chemistry* was published as a paperback original. It garnered, however, many more reviews, including one by Molly Antopol in *Southern Review* that praised the realism of Rash's dialogue and his "mastery of character" in the "meticulously constructed tales."[26] Another reviewer remarked that "each story is poetic and carefully crafted"; a third concurred, calling the stories "tightly spun" and "evocative."[27] None of the reviewers, as noted earlier, seemed aware of *Casualties* as the source of nearly two-thirds of the book's selections, and thus none commented on the types of revisions Rash had made in preparing them for reprinting. Although space limitations preclude detailed discussion of those revisions, readers interested in Rash's writing process would do well to compare the original and reprinted stories' opening and closing paragraphs. The majority of the changes, however, are not substantive but stylistic, creating greater economy of expression by deleting unnecessary repetition or unneeded modifiers, by omitting stale or unoriginal similes ("brittle as thin ice"), and by substituting one word for two or three (thus "without humor" becomes "humorlessly"). Rash also uses more contractions in the revised first-person narratives, rendering their tone more conversational, and adds instances of colloquial dialogue, as when Mrs. Triplett in "Cold Harbor" says about her wounded son's condition not "it's made me nothing more than a bitter old woman" (*Casualties* 55) but rather "it's done made me bitter" (*Chemistry* 104). One of the most striking changes in this story is Rash's greater use of that son's former nurse's first name: whereas in *Casualties* Anna's name does not appear until the third page of the story, it occurs in the opening paragraph of the revision in *Chemistry* and again in that version's fourth paragraph. Rash also calls Anna's previously unnamed husband Jonathon. Such changes tend to generate greater engagement with the characters. Other revisions in these stories are meant to clarify transitions or to demarcate more clearly, through the insertion of additional spacing, individual scenes or climactic episodes. At times, too, a revision makes a character's motives more ambiguous, less narrowly delimited, as when Rash deletes Anna's desire not to bring a child into the postwar world, the seeming explanation for her marriage's failure in the original version of "Cold Harbor." That omission makes the impact of the war on her psyche more comprehensive, less neatly analyzable.

In contrast to *Casualties,* which opens and closes with stories set in Watauga County in earlier eras, *Chemistry* begins and ends with selections set in other western North Carolina counties at a time closer to today. The Tuckasegee River of "Their Ancient, Glittering Eyes" flows through Jackson County, where Rash teaches at Western Carolina University, and he opens *Chemistry* with what one reviewer calls "perhaps Rash's funniest story," which begins as an apparent tall tale but soon becomes a testimony to the experience of mystery, both natural and supernatural.[28] The story takes its title from the final line of Yeats's 1936 poem "Lapis Lazuli," a work that contrasts the tragic and comic dimensions of human experience and the divergent responses to the former. In a world threatened by bombs dropped from "Aeroplane and Zeppelin," Yeats contends, poets affirm life by maintaining hope, by remaining confident that "all things fall and are built again, / And those that build them again are gay." Similarly the three "Chinamen" whom the poem's speaker observes on a lapis lazuli sculpture follow an ascending path toward a place of rest from which "on all the tragic scene they stare." Yet amid the "mournful melodies" that one requests, "their ancient, glittering eyes," writes Yeats, "are gay," paradoxically joyful despite human suffering.[29]

Rash's protagonists, octogenarians Rudisell and Campbell and a septuagenarian, Creech, are an unlikely trio who frequent a country store called Riverside Gas and Grocery. Their explanations for the contemporary world's "devolution" are broadly comic, the octogenarians blaming Franklin Roosevelt and fluoridated water, Creech indicting Elvis Presley and television.[30] As the story unfolds, however, these "ancients" assume heroic qualities, moving from their initial skepticism about the report they hear of a monstrous fish in the Tuckasegee—"like a alligator but for the fins," as one fisherman declares—to certainty even when the condescending game warden doubts their testimony (4). Rash heightens the story's humorous tone by offering comic catalogs of the various lures people use to try to capture this lunker and of the specimens caught, which include, among assorted species of fish, "one ball cap, . . . one old boot . . . [and] a gray squirrel" (10). After weeks of futile attempts by others, the old men eventually identify the fish that has eluded them: a sturgeon more than six feet long, a species "once in near every river, but now endangered," that they learn of from the local library's copy of *Freshwater Fish of North America* (18). Borrowing deep-sea fishing gear from Jarvis Hampton, whose surname also appears in Rash's first two books of stories, and using a water snake as bait, the men get the fish to strike, Ru-disell having tied a hay hook to his right hand with baling twine, a weapon with which he intends to gaff "the behemoth" (18), as does the ill-fated fish-erman in Rash's poem "Blue Cat" in *Waking*. Though Rudisell makes one ineffective stab at the sturgeon, he later aims the hay hook so that it cuts the fish free, an action approved by Campbell, who says, "You done the right thing" (20). The men are pleased with the outcome of their confrontation with the fish. Unlike Hemingway's Santiago in *The Old Man and the Sea,* these ancients experience no pyrrhic victory, towing a skeleton ashore. Their emotion is one of joy, not stoicism, for they have valued the integrity of this creature—and by extension of nature itself.

Rash imbues this tale with a religious dimension in several ways. His choice of the term *behemoth* to describe the fish may be meant to recall God's command to Job: "Behold behemoth which I made" (Job 40:15 [RSV]). But Rash also includes such words as *vigil* (5, 12) and *heretically* (12) and refers to the trio of men as "old-world saints" in the story's final sentence: "Com-ing out of the shadows, they blinked their eyes as if dazzled, much in the manner of old-world saints who have witnessed the blinding brilliance of the one true vision" (22). Rash does not elaborate on the content of that vision, but it implicitly involves renunciation of humanity's power to destroy nature wantonly. The sturgeon is itself a figure of heroic strength and antiquity, displaying "an array of rusting hooks and lures that hung from the lips like medals" (19). Initially during the time the men strive to locate and identify it, the fish also represents spiritual mystery, for, like theologians of the *via negativa,* "of species they could speak only by negation" (6).

The most significant image in this story, beyond the fish itself, is a scute, one of the armor-like plates covering the sturgeon's body that Rudisell finds in the river, an object he considers "better than gold," in part because it will help prove to the skeptical game warden Meekins the identity of the elu-sive fish (21). "He held it eye level in front of Meekins's face," Rash writes, "as if it were a silty monocle they both might peer through" (21). But the game warden remains cynical and supercilious, blind to the import of the old men's actions despite the scute's potential as an instrument of vision. Rash's story itself, however, fulfills that role for the reader, heightening re-spect for nature's mysterious reality independent of human needs and desires. Because in *Chemistry* the collection's title story immediately follows "Their Ancient, Glittering Eyes," readers encounter two tales in succession intended to enlarge the scope of their vision, the opening story by foregrounding an unusual encounter with nature, the title story by highlighting hunger for the

spiritual, for the *super*natural. One of Emerson's observations in his essay
Nature is apropos here: "Idealism is a hypothesis to account for nature by
other principles than those of carpentry and chemistry."[31]

Another of the new stories in *Chemistry*, "Blackberries in June," is linked
to these first two by its water imagery, for the young marrieds, Jamie and
Matt, who are its central characters, live at a lake house and enjoy making
love in the lake, where they experience what Matt thinks of as "the unburdening of water" and Jamie envisions as being "unchained in the weightless-
ness of water" (63, 54). A third-person narrative told from Jamie's point of
view, this story demonstrates Rash's ability to limn the competing allegiances
involved in moral choices and the intricate set of forces that helps to shape a
person's life. When Jamie's older brother, Charlton, who has been employing
Matt on generous terms that have enabled the couple to purchase the lake
house, loses his leg in a logging accident, Jamie's mother asks her daughter
and Matt to sacrifice the house to aid Charlton and his family. Matt, who
believes "you make your own luck" (62), argues that they should keep their
home because "this house is going to save us a lot of money, money we can
help them with later" (70). Although Jamie yields to this rationalization, the
story's closing image suggests that she is not wholly persuaded by it.

"Deep Gap," another of the book's new stories, portrays some of the
major ways in which contemporary Appalachia is being transformed, most
notably by drug addiction and by land developers. Much of this story's
power derives from its tightly limited focus on the relationship of Marshall
Vaughn to his son Brad, whom the father tries to rescue from drugs. The
owner of a hardware store that has been in the family for three generations,
Marshall had removed Brad at gunpoint, six months before the story's present time, from an apartment in Charlotte, bringing him back to Deep Gap,
the actual name of a community in Watauga County but a place name that
also becomes symbolic of the painful chasm that has opened up between
father and son—and between the traditional Appalachia of Marshall's up-
bringing and the modern Appalachia of Brad's addiction. In the story's climactic scene, Brad's relapse thrusts an anguished Marshall into such despair
that he proposes both he and Brad commit suicide, for Marshall recognizes,
as Rash does, the self-destructiveness of drug abuse. "Don't you even care
that you're killing yourself?" Marshall had asked Brad on the drive from
Charlotte to Deep Gap, realizing that this eventuality is precisely what awaits
Brad as the story draws to its close (150). But instead of accepting his father's
proposal, Brad decides, "I want to get better," a response Marshall knows
will complicate, not simplify, their lives (161). In a reversal of the episode in
the *Aeneid* in which Aeneas carries his father, Anchises, away from burning

Troy, the sixty-year-old Marshall carries Brad (who has been severely beaten because of unpaid drug debts) out of the trailer where his son has been living to drive him to a nearby hospital, "a place where the injured came to be healed," in the story's final words (162). Whether such healing will occur remains uncertain, as is often the case in Rash's stories, the deep gap of the title reminiscent of the flaws in human nature that lead Tracy in Rash's first collection to assume that people live in "a fallen world." "Deep Gap" poignantly portrays Marshall's sense of loss and disillusionment amid the cultural transformation and personal pain he experiences. Listening to the radio, he hears an archaeologist say, "Cultures disappear, are replaced by other cultures, and that's as it should be" (157). But this story challenges so simplistic an assumption. "Deep Gap" articulates Rash's judgment that the so-called drug culture is no substitute for traditional mountain culture but is instead its scourge.

Current readers of "Pemberton's Bride" and "Speckled Trout" are likely to be interested in them less as independent pieces of fiction and more as precursors to the novels into which they were incorporated. "Speckled Trout," first published in the *Kenyon Review* and the recipient of an O. Henry Award, underwent fewer revisions in becoming the opening chapter of *The World Made Straight*, although in its original form the story makes no reference to the elder Toomey's cutting the protagonist's Achilles tendon with a knife. In "Speckled Trout" that protagonist is called Lanny Burgess rather than Travis Shelton, and the elder Toomey is Linwood, not Carlton. The former schoolteacher who purchases marijuana plants that Lanny steals from the Toomeys is named Leonard Hamby, not Shuler, a renaming that underscores Leonard's role as mentor to Travis because the German noun *Schule* means "school." But that renaming also indicates Leonard's own need for development because in German *Schüler* means "schoolboy" or "pupil" as well as "scholar." The drug-addicted young woman who lives at Leonard's trailer is named Wendy rather than Dena, as in the novel, a name change that may be related to the German verb *dienen*, "to serve, to be useful," a semi-ironic etymology, because Dena is both a servant to her addictions and almost useless in assisting others. The Dobermans that Leonard owns in the short story become Plott hounds in the novel, a bear-hunting breed associated with Appalachian culture in John Ehle's novels as well.

"Pemberton's Bride," more novella than short story, covers a far more extended period of time than "Speckled Trout," providing an overview of the novel *Serena*. As with "Speckled Trout," Rash makes several name changes in moving from one text to the other, including altering Sarah Harmon's first name to Rachel and calling her child Jacob rather than Esau. Perhaps the most significant alteration from novella to novel occurs, however, in the way Rash has the conflict between Serena and Sarah culminate. In the novella Serena and her henchman Chaney (the novel's Galloway) murder Sarah and Esau, while in the novel Rachel and Jacob escape. Whereas the novella ends with Pemberton cleaning the bloodstained knife his wife used and putting it away, the novel concludes with Pemberton's murder, arranged by Serena and presided over by Galloway, and with Jacob's vengeance on Serena and Galloway years later in Brazil. But both accounts of Serena emphasize her heartlessness, ambition, and pride. "Pemberton's Bride" is the most episodic of the fictions published in *Chemistry,* yet its portrait of Serena and her intense relationship with Pemberton, along with the violence of its events, especially the killing of Sarah's father in the opening scene, is utterly compelling.

In concluding *Chemistry* with "Speckled Trout," Rash gives the collection greater coherence by returning to a story involving fishing, at least in part, as does the book's opening tale. He also helps to unify the book by presenting "Speckled Trout" as another story that turns on the characters' moral choices, as do "Blackberries in June," "Overtime," "Honesty," "The Projectionist's Wife," and "Deep Gap." Moreover the water imagery in "Speckled Trout" ties this story to several others already discussed, including "Cold Harbor," which Rash placed at the center of this new collection, the seventh of its thirteen stories. Only in "Their Ancient, Glittering Eyes" is the tone predominantly humorous. In most of the other selections, the characters make painful discoveries about themselves or others, as does the narrator of "Honesty," who recognizes and confesses that he is not a good person, and as does Jamie of "Blackberries in June," who at story's end faces her image in a mirror on which "a crack jagged across the glass like a lightning bolt, a crack caulk couldn't fill" (71), the simile indicative of divine condemnation of Jamie and her husband's decision. The characters' plights are sometimes unresolved, as in "Cold Harbor," "Dangerous Love," and "Deep Gap"—or resolved but still painful, as in "Last Rite." But like the old men of "Their Ancient, Glittering Eyes" and like the figures on Yeats's piece of lapis lazuli, Rash's characters in these stories generally confront life's challenges and disappointments with dignity and courage.

CHAPTER 3

Eureka Mill, Among the Believers, Raising the Dead, and *Waking*

Early in his career, Rash received wider recognition as a poet than as a fiction writer. By the time his first novel appeared in 2002, he had already published three books of poems: *Eureka Mill* (1998), *Among the Believers* (2000), and *Raising the Dead* (2002), each of them given several laudatory reviews, the second with an introduction by poet Anthony Hecht praising the collection as an "extraordinary volume of poems" that Hecht found "uniformly and unfalteringly . . . excellent."[1] To these three volumes Rash added *Waking* in 2011. This chapter will examine Rash's achievement in poetry, a genre about which he has said, "It has a way of making things unforgettable. . . . When it's done right, it's the ultimate form of writing."[2]

As a poet Rash has written effectively in traditional forms, free verse, and syllabics, his preferred form in *Among the Believers* and subsequent collections being the seven-syllable line derived from Welsh poetry. Like many other southern poets, he relies heavily on narrative, though he is equally adept in lyric modes when he chooses and frequently creates poems with a strong elegiac tone. One of his principal aims, he notes, is accessibility: "One thing I admire in poetry and that I love about Appalachian poetry in particular is that the Appalachian poet is often a poet whose writing is accessible, very concrete, and yet there's an amazing depth to it. . . . It's the poetry I find in Robert Frost, in Seamus Heaney. It's a multi-layered poetry but with a surface accessibility."[3] Frost and Heaney are two of Rash's most important poetic influences, as are Robert Morgan, Fred Chappell, and Jeff Daniel Marion, among contemporary poets from Appalachia.

The prominent subjects in Rash's fiction likewise appear in his poetry—family ties and family conflicts, love, death, the challenges and exploitation experienced by working-class people, the difficulties and satisfactions of agrarian life, the wonders and terrors of nature—but in contrast to his fiction, Rash's poetry is far more autobiographical, more personal. The *I* of his poems is often, though hardly invariably—and especially not in *Eureka Mill*—the poet himself, with no intent on Rash's part to create personae or establish a gap between the poet and the poem's speaker. Yet as poems such as "A Preacher Who Takes up Serpents Laments the Presence of Skeptics in His Church" and "Black-Eyed Susans" demonstrate, he can create powerful dramatic monologues in the voices of invented characters, a skill honed by his fiction writing and by his artistic commitment to Keatsian negative capability, "that idea," as Rash explained to an interviewer, "of entering another consciousness but also entering another voice," a quality he claims for his poetry as well as his fiction.[4]

Such negative capability is amply apparent in *Eureka Mill*, a collection of forty poems that focuses on his grandparents' generation and their experience of Appalachian outmigration from the mountains of North Carolina to the mill town of Chester, South Carolina. While the book deals, then, with the poet's family history, these poems also offer a broader social portrait of people being uprooted, of the transition from an agrarian to an industrial economy. Randall Wilhelm calls *Eureka Mill* "Rash's most overtly political book," and another critic describes it as "an exploration of a universal condition, displacement, in term of Rash's own family history."[5] Behind the mill of this book's title lie William Blake's "dark satanic mills."[6] Moreover the past Rash invokes here is not primarily his own but that of other family members and the entire mill community, as well as the past documented by social historians and such reformers as photographer Lewis Hine, who is mentioned by name in one poem and alluded to in another. Rash's interest in the past and its ongoing impact, an interest that also pervades his fiction, is announced in the book's epigraph from Frank Tannenbaum's *Darker Phases of the South*, which describes the mill worker's house as "a spiritual grave" and the mill village as "a spiritual cemetery" that "buries its inhabitants and hides them from the world."[7] Yet while Rash, like Tannenbaum, critiques the destructive effects of mill life, he also takes pains to depict the ways in which the mill workers were more than mere victims. Without idealizing or sentimentalizing them, the poet celebrates their humanity and their resistance to economic exploitation.

Although *Eureka Mill* was Rash's first book of poems, it reveals an author highly skilled in traditional forms such as blank verse, other iambic meters, and both exact and slant rhymes. Three of the poems employ the midline break of Anglo-Saxon verse and some of that verse form's pronounced alliteration across the two halves of a line. One poem is an Italian sonnet (32), and another, "In a Dry Time," is an iambic tetrameter villanelle disguised by its lack of stanza divisions (9). Divided into six untitled sections of varying numbers of poems, the book opens and closes with two italicized selections, *"Invocation"* and *"Last Words,"* that serve as prologue and epilogue. In the former Rash invokes the spirit of his dead grandfather, buried back in Buncombe County, whom he lures with a mason jar lid filled with moonshine:

> *Grandfather guide my hand*
> *to weave with words a thread*
> *of truth as I write down*
> *your life and other lives,*
> *close kin but strangers too,*
> *those lives all lived as gears*
> *in Springs' cotton mill*
> *and let me not forget*
> *your lives were more than that.* (xv–xvi)

The brevity of these iambic trimeter lines may be meant to reflect the strict limitations imposed on these workers' lives, just as the absence of rhyme suggests the disharmonious relation of worker to employer. In *"Last Words,"* in contrast, the grandfather himself speaks in a fluid, conversational blank verse, absolving his grandson of further obligations to him and humorously urging the poet, *"Take a B.C. Powder, get some sleep. / I know too well the sun hits like a hammer / when it rises up after a moonshine night"* (63). That moonshine refers both to the alcohol the poet's grandfather loved and to the moonlight of poetic inspiration, of the imagination's creative powers exercised by Rash himself.

One of the most striking features of *Eureka Mill* is Rash's use of first-person plural speakers. More than a third of the book's poems utilize *we* as their narrative point of view, thus stressing the importance of solidarity to these workers as well as the commitment to community among Appalachian people, who are often stereotyped as isolated individualists. Although the first poem in part 1, "Eureka," mentions the poet's illiterate paternal grandfather and his annual repainting of that word on the mill's water tower, none of the other poems in parts 1 and 2 refer explicitly to the grandfather. Not until part 3, which contains just four poems, is he again the focus of the book. Instead Rash provides a group portrait of the mill workers and of their representative experiences as one-time farmers failing to thrive in agriculture and as factory hands subjected to monotonous labor and dangerous work conditions, including child labor in "The Sweeper," a first-person singular poem in iambic tetrameter quatrains rhymed *aabb,* with most of the rhymes slant to reflect the dissonance of the child's life (19). This poem draws on Blake's "The Chimney Sweep" in its depiction of exploited child labor as one species of social and economic injustice. While other poems in parts 1 and 2 use first-person singular speakers whose experiences may be similar to Rash's grandfather's, those speakers are never identified as the grandfather. Rash thus presents a wide-ranging set of speakers, both male and female, of narrative points of view, of stanza structures, and of metrical forms that engage the reader's interest and keep the book's chronicling of the workers' lives varied and fresh. Irony is one of Rash's main literary devices, as when "Eureka," a title that implies the thrill of discovery, opens with the line "Here was no place   for illumination" and later states that "lost wages or fingers" were "the risk of reflection" (3). Nor does Rash idealize either agrarian life or the mill workers themselves, as poems such as "Drought" and "Tobacco" (the latter revised and reprinted in *Waking*), along with "Fighting Gamecocks" and "Boundaries," attest.

The book is ordered chronologically, starting with the disillusioned farmers' arrival at the mill in the second decade of the twentieth century and moving forward to the 1950s and the poet's grandfather's death when Rash was five years old. By repeating some of the workers' names in several different poems, Rash reinforces the sense of community the book offers and tightens its focus. The poet's historical consciousness reaches a crescendo in part 4 with poems set in the late 1920s and 1930s amid the struggle to unionize the mills. "The Ballad of Ella Mae Wiggins" recounts the 1929 murder of the figure named in the title, a union organizer at the Loray Mill in Gastonia. Wiggins had five children and was also a songwriter, "A Mill Mother's Lament" being her best-known composition. No one was ever convicted of her murder. "Flying Squadron," a term that refers to traveling groups of union supporters, alludes to the violence in Honea Path, South Carolina, in 1934 when six striking pickets were shot to death and more than twenty others wounded. Yet despite such blatant evidence of social and economic injustice, the workers at Eureka Mill remain conflicted, as Rash portrays them in "1934," for "Old Man Springs" had kept the mill running, its workers employed, even when "the other mills laid off." And so in the poem's final quatrain,

> When a flying squadron headed south
> and crossed the Chester County line,

> we left our shift to walk outside.
> We filled our fists to welcome them. (39)

Those raised fists are both a sign of solidarity and a threat to the union or-
ganizers and are thus an apt emblem of these workers' ambivalence. Rash
allows Colonel Springs to speak for himself in a later poem in part 5, "Last
Interview," another of the collection's poems in blank verse, in which Springs
appeals to the principle of noblesse oblige and refers disparagingly to the
Vanderbilt agrarians (52). Part 5 concludes with the Colonel's funeral and
his son-in-law's ordering the workers to return to the mill.

   Part 6, like part 3, comprises poems about the poet's family members,
and like part 3 it includes only four poems, a number that again mirrors the
poet's intent to make the book primarily social history, not simply family
history. In the opening poem of this final section, "First Shift" (and in this
section's other three poems), Rash speaks of himself for the first time since
"*Invocation*," describing his grandparents' and father's passage through the
mill's gate, "where I cannot follow, / except in blood-memory, except in the
knowledge / I eat well and I rest on the gift of their labors" (57). The poet's
heartfelt gratitude to his ancestors is one of the main motives for his writing,
in this book and others. That sense of gratitude prompts both recollection
of his family's past and exploration of Appalachian history and culture. The
term *blood-memory* is one that reappears in *Raising the Dead* (56) and *Waking* (24), where it suggests not only ancestral but also cultural memory, at
times memory tied to Appalachian or Welsh traditions, at other times to a
Jungian collective unconscious rife with archetypal images and experiences
common to all human beings. Rash has identified himself as a Jungian and
has said that "really good" writers move beyond local color "into that collective unconscious, into the Jungian realm."[8]

   The second and third poems in part 6 depict, respectively, the poet ex-
amining photos of his parents and of his grandfather: the former shows his
father with his "back against the [mill's] chain-link fence," hand meshed
in the fence "as if / caught in a sprung-steel grip," in the poem's closing
words (58); the latter photo includes the poet himself and several of his
grandfather's friends who had gathered to share their tales of a day's successful fishing. Through these photos Rash establishes continuity across the
generations—the photographs, like his poems, affirming interconnection.
The same is true of the final poem in part 6, "July, 1949," one of the book's
most poignant texts. "This is what I cannot remember," the poem begins,
as Rash describes his mother's departure from Watauga County for Chester
some four years before his birth, his inability to remember highlighting the

importance of both collective memory transmitted by family storytelling or such artifacts as photographs and the reconstructive powers of the historical/ creative imagination itself. The final stanza of this free-verse poem reads:

> She is dreaming another life,
> young enough to believe
> it can only be better—
> indoor plumbing, eight hour shifts, a man
> who waits unknowing for her, a man
> who cannot hear through the weave room's
> roar the world's soft click,
> fate's tumblers falling into place,
> soft as the sound of my mother's
> bare feet as she runs,
> runs toward him, toward me. (62)

The enjambment in lines 4–6 and line 9, along with the poet's insistent use of repetition, propels the stanza's forward momentum, adding to the urgency and seemingly inevitable outcome of the young woman's running, which becomes in the final line less a flight from the past and more a flight toward a future that encompasses both the poet's father and the poet himself. Although nearly a decade would elapse, Rash's parents would ultimately escape the mill's grip for careers as teachers.

In *Eureka Mill,* thanks to Rash's eye for vivid and appropriate details and for telling incidents, the poems regularly achieve the sense of discovery, of revelation, to which the term *eureka* is the proverbial response. One reviewer spoke of the book's "original and memorable poetry," while another referred to "the consistent excellence of these poems" and to Rash's "mastery of craft."[9] Throughout the book the poet's diction is forceful and exact, yet accessible. It is especially notable for its strong verbs: "*I unscrew the mason jar, / pool the lid with moonshine, / flare the battered cigarette lighter*" (xv). Thematically *Eureka Mill* exemplifies its author's characteristic concern for the potential erasure of Appalachian culture: as Ronald Eller points out in *Miners, Millhands, and Mountaineers,* "For over three-quarters of a million mountaineers, the migration from mountain cabin to mill village was a major break with their land, their families, and their culture."[10]

Rash's interest in preserving that culture is readily apparent in his second collection of poems, *Among the Believers,* which has as its epigraph a quotation from fellow mountain poet George Scarbrough's "Summer Revival": "Let me forget nothing now / In this hour of losing."[11] The book is dedicated "In Memory of my father James Hubert Rash—believer" (vii). While religious belief is the most prominent type of belief presented in the book, the poems address other kinds of belief as well, including superstitions based on folklore and, as in "Catamount," convictions based on personal experience rather than conventional wisdom or even scientific consensus. Political beliefs are largely absent, though political allegiances figure significantly in two poems that deal with the Shelton Laurel massacre in Madison County during the Civil War. The volume is divided into five untitled parts of uneven lengths, with narrative poems predominating. This is Rash's first collection using the seven-syllable line that has remained a staple of his poetry, a structure borrowed from the ancient Welsh poetic form known as *awdl gywydd*. About this form Rash has said, "It seems to fit the stark world I write about. I also love the sound intensity of Welsh poetry," which relies heavily on internal rhymes, alliteration, assonance, and consonance.[12] In his late twenties, Rash reports, he did "an intense study of traditional Welsh poetics" and began to incorporate its interwoven aural features into his own poetry.[13] Of the seven-syllable line he remarks, "I think I was wired for this line form. It gives a narrative poet something solid to stand on, but also it makes you be concise."[14] The enjambment that results, moreover, from so short a line contributes to his poems' narrative momentum, as does his tendency to write many single-sentence and two-sentence poems.

"Decoration Day" exhibits several of the traits mentioned above, including its focus on the southern custom of honoring the dead by having kinfolk gather to clean community or family gravesites once each year, usually in late spring or summer. But Rash's poem gains greater intensity by honing in on a very specific practice: an artist's drawing portraits from photographs.

> One whose hand could make a face
> out of paper and pencil
> would lay the glassed black and whites
> on the communion table,
> trace our dead kin back to life
> to walk this land they once walked
> and see again, through our eyes,
> the dogwoods, ash trees, and oaks,
> swift flowing creeks, narrow skies,
> peaks and coves in memory mapped
> so deep not even heaven
> could wish them from looking back. (21)

The pronounced alliteration and assonance in this poem begin with the *d*s and long *a*s of its title, with the hard *c* of *Decoration* also recurring throughout the poem, notably in its final word. Long *es* and *is* augment the poem's aural power, as does the *n* first used in *Decoration* and *One,* the last syllable of the former rhyming with the poem's first word. Such density of sound effects, which extends to the end rhyme occurring in lines 7 and 9, is characteristic of Rash's work and helps explain some of the emotional impact his poems have, as well as why he has said that his poems usually undergo "anywhere from twenty to forty" drafts.[15] Rash's diction in this poem is typically simple and direct, relying exclusively on monosyllables in four of the first six lines. Like the artist whose skill "trace[s] our dead kin back to life," Rash seeks to recover the lost lineaments of his ancestors and of the vanishing culture that shaped them. The poet's use of a first-person plural speaker here reinforces the sense of community the poem conveys. In "Decoration Day" past and present generations meet at this "communion table" in a sacrament of com-memoration, the dead revivified to see the beauty of the natural world again through the eyes of the living.

In many respects, however, *Among the Believers* is a death-haunted book in which the hope of resurrection is severely muted. As Hecht notes in his introductory essay, "the general tone of these poems is somber and some-times stark" (xiv). Of the thirteen poems in part 1, for example, at least ten deal directly with death; almost all of those in part 3 address this subject, as do all nine of the poems in part 5. Moreover graveyards are one of the book's principal settings. The southern gothic tradition, with its interest in the violent and the grotesque, inspires several of these poems, as it does some of Rash's fiction. The book's second poem, "The Skeleton in the Dogwood," for instance, centers on an image to which Rash returns in *One Foot in Eden* when Holland Winchester's body is hidden among the branches of a white oak, concealed there for nearly two decades.

The book's initial poem, "On the Border," introduces the theme of mor-tality by portraying a "hard country, / bare hills, dark valleys, gray juts / of stone" that could as easily be southern Appalachia as the borderlands be-tween England and Scotland in which the poem is actually set. "Here," Rash writes, "men argued map lines with blood, // raised death like a seed crop" (3). From these generalizations about the land's inhabitants, and drawing on an incident reported in David Fischer's *Albion's Seed,* the poet narrows his lens to recount the deaths of a band of reivers who drown trying to carry their plunder across a river ironically named Eden. Liminal spaces are a re-curring motif in Rash's work, as his short story "Between the States" and the opening scene of *Saints at the River* also indicate. The border Rash depicts in this poem is more than geographical; it also marks the boundary between humane and inhumane conduct (the "murders, rapes, // burned homesteads,

ransacked churches" mentioned earlier in the poem) and the boundaries between life and death, time and eternity. As this poem points out, human beings
dwell in a post-Edenic world.

The historical perspective Rash adopts in "On the Border" recurs in
"The Skeleton in the Dogwood," which is identified in parentheses as set in
"Watauga County, 1895" (4). In this second collection of poems, then, Rash
immediately declares his allegiance to western North Carolina and to a consciousness of its past. Four other poems in this book have dates in their titles,
and three name Watauga or Madison Counties in those titles. Western North
Carolina place names—Boone, Asheville, Bryson City—and references to
Buncombe County and assorted rivers and creeks in the region fill the poems.
Rash thus grounds his work in specific times, places, people, and events. Although death presides over many of the poems, he presents this subject with
the "versatility, amplitude" that Hecht found so attractive a trait of the book
(xv). The varied narratives Rash offers are dramatic and suspenseful, and
the economy with which they are told (only three of the volume's fifty-four
poems run longer than a page, and many are scarcely half a page in length)
adds to their power. "Scarecrow" and "The Corpse Bird," two of the best
poems in part 1, are twelve and ten lines, respectively, the former consisting
of three quatrains rhymed *abcb* and the latter of a single stanza, and both
employ lines of seven syllables with a single exception: the first line of the
third stanza in "Scarecrow," a line that also contains the poem's only word
of more than one or two syllables.

As in "On the Border," Rash underscores the cruelty of human nature
in later poems in part 1, though nature itself is also seen as lethal in "Scarecrow" and "Flood" and in "Graveyard Fields," which concludes part 2.
"The Confession" relates the story of an unnamed woman who "hacked
the throat of her child / with a knife more rust than steel," this poem's
twenty-six lines skillfully shaped into a single suspenseful sentence (9). Both
"Madison County: 1864" and "Allen's Command" record what Rash calls
in the former "an intimate politics / of atrocity," the Shelton Laurel massacre
of January 1863 (and its aftermath), during which thirteen suspected Union
sympathizers were executed in cold blood (11). "Those fortunate," Rash
states, "died from musket balls, the rest / hoe-hacked like snakes" (12). The
youngest victim, David Shelton, was thirteen years old. Rash has written at
least three short essays discussing this massacre, noting an ancestor's possible
role in it and reminding readers that residents of the mountain South often
supported the Union and that he thus had kin who fought on both sides during the Civil War. The community of Aho, near his maternal grandmother's
farm, was "a Unionist hotbed," he remarks, while Madison County, where

some of his father's ancestors lived, "was evenly split between Unionists and Confederates."[16] This massacre is also the subject of poems in *Raising the Dead* and *Waking,* and it plays a central role in Rash's third novel, *The World Made Straight.*

All the poems in part 2 of *Among the Believers* incorporate religious settings, individuals, or subject matter such as foot washing, speaking in tongues, and providential interpretations of events. Two are dramatic monologues spoken by preachers, including this section's compelling opening poem, "A Preacher Who Takes up Serpents Laments the Presence of Skeptics in His Church." This poem complicates the reader's response to the theme of death presented in part 1 because this preacher insists that "a man afraid to die cannot live" and rejects the nonbeliever's assumption that "death is an end," this claim itself a profession of belief (19). Rash assigns to this preacher the poet's own ecological concerns when the preacher observes, "Less than a mile from here / the stench of sulpher rises / like fog off the Pigeon River" (19). "They cannot see," he continues, "a river / is a vein in God's arm" (19). So successfully does Rash immerse his readers in this preacher's viewpoint that they cannot ignore its claims and must consider the book's other poems on death—at least in part—from the religious perspective the preacher articulates.

The poems of part 2 involve religious concerns prevalent throughout Rash's career, delineating moments of intersection between the human and the divine. Rash shares British and American romanticism's assumption that nature can be an instrument of spiritual revelation. In "Foot Washing," for instance, he notes how "spring's warm light / falls like grace through willow leaves, / golds the river" (23), and in "The Language of Canaan," he upholds Emerson's confidence in nature itself as a species of divine speech:

> If dawn caught and dazzled on
> dew beads strung to spider's web,
> sweep of shadow crossed meadow
> like calming hand, it might come—
> luxuriant bloom of assurance
> grafted onto tongue, language
> graced with a cadence so pure
> ears deaf a lifetime now heard,
> and for decades afterward
> whole settlements would visit
> streamside, meadow, that place one
> world bled into another. (24)

Such intermingling of the physical and spiritual sanctifies nature, transfiguring it into the Promised Land of the Israelites. The ecstatic moment of revelation here is marked by a lengthening to nine syllables of the poem's seven-syllable norm: the line "luxuriant bloom of assurance" itself involves a metaphor drawn from the natural world. While nature is often terrifyingly destructive in Rash's work, as in the snowstorm that kills four hundred cattle in "Graveyard Fields," it can also testify to the presence of the divine and to humanity's crucial dependence on a physical world beyond humankind's making.

A noteworthy feature of Rash's diction in this volume, one that has become increasingly prominent in his work, is his use of hyphenated compound nouns reminiscent of the kenning in Anglo-Saxon poetry. In fact, in "Animal Hides," the poet refers to hunters as "death-hurriers / [who] kenned animal once meant soul," his choice of verb indicating this coined term's link to such familiar kennings as "whale-road" (34). In the same poem Rash includes the hyphenated nouns *barn-back, shed-side, wind-lift, fur-scrap,* and *pelt-shadow,* terms that lend his lines solidity and physicality and suggest an earlier era in human history and poetry. At other times Rash omits the hyphen and creates compound nouns more typical of German than English: *floor-stone, gutterswell,* and *springflow* in "In a Springhouse at Night" (45). All these terms add vividness and variety to his diction along with concreteness, making readers alert to the resistance the poet meets when, for example, he "wade[s] through thorn-snatch" to reach an abandoned well (48).

Unlike parts 1 and 3, part 4 is unified not primarily by death imagery but by imagery of water, although water itself had already appeared as an instrument of death in the book's opening poem, in "Flood," in "North of Asheville," and in the snowstorm of "Graveyard Fields." Yet for Christians, in the sacrament of baptism, water becomes a means of rebirth, as Rash explained in a 2006 interview with Thomas Bjerre. In that same interview he also pointed out that "in Welsh and Celtic folklore, water is a conduit between the living and the dead."[17] Part 4 includes the poem "Blue River," which describes a church mural of the River Jordan painted by the poet's father. That biblical river was the site of Jesus' baptism, and it also marks the traditional boundary between this world and heaven's Promised Land. Rash concludes the poem by calling this church's baptismal pool the place where he would soon be "washed away in a current / raised by my father's right hand" (46). Even though Rash does not capitalize *father* in this passage, the reader might well detect an intentional ambiguity here, an invoking of God as spiritual parent. Nevertheless several of the poems in this section simply present physical deaths rather than mirroring the death-and-rebirth motif evident in "Blue River" and implicit in three consecutive poems about the poet's maternal grandfather's death in July 1959. The first of these poems ends with an allusion to Welshman Henry Vaughan's "They Are All Gone into the World of Light" (54), and the third ends with a reference to "that word the preacher spoke" at the grandfather's funeral, a word that echoes in the child-poet's mind, "as though the writing spider / has caught time, suspended there / between an E and a Y," the word being *eternity* (56).

It is in "Morning Service: August, 1959," however, the final poem in part 4, that Rash provides this section's most forceful testimony to life beyond the grave.[18] He has spoken of this poem as recording the "first moment in my recognition of timelessness, transcendence, . . . what Wordsworth called 'spots of time,' living in the eternal."[19] Set shortly after his grandfather's death, the poem depicts the impact of his great-aunt's a cappella hymn singing on the child-poet. This aunt is an artist figure whose song, like the poet's own, witnesses to the resurrection power of both humanity and divinity. The control exercised by the poet over the poem's closing sentence, which runs to more than sixteen lines, gives credibility to the claim that "she led us across Jordan, / and the gravestones leaned as if / even the dead were listening" (59). Part of the potency of that final sentence derives from the poet's quick glance into his aunt's future to the moment when a stroke "wrenched her / face into a gnarled silence" (59). Yet without denying the destructiveness of time, the poet affirms the potential for rebirth in eternity.

Despite the hopefulness apparent in this poem, however, all nine of the poems in part 5 involve death and loss, a theme evident in this section's initial poem, "Abandoned Homestead in Watauga County," and reinforced by the westward movement of the speaker in the book's final poem. Part 5 inventories all sorts of losses: the decay of a plank bridge, the burial of a cousin's father, the submersion of a church in "Beneath Keowee" (an artificial lake in upstate South Carolina), the death in childbirth of a great-aunt and her baby, the gaunt visage of a crucified Christ painted by the poet's father. Rash offers no easy answers to the questions posed by death. The burden of mortality remains problematic, as he intimates when he concludes the poem about his great-aunt's death in childbirth with this image from a photo of her lying in her coffin: "a cross of shadow, shadowing death, / across an uncomprehending face" (70). Rash mentions cemeteries in nearly half the poems in part 5, making the reader intensely aware of death's wide reach. But he also writes of "fog lift[ing]" off a stream "like risen souls" in one of those poems about graveyards (68) and speaks in another of "vision beyond human measure" (69), a phrase that testifies to the limits of human knowledge and to the mysterious depths of human existence. For Rash, as he once said to an interviewer, "an important value of art is 'to deepen the mystery.'" In fact he went on to explain his use of Appalachian folklore, which appears in several poems in this collection, in terms of "the sense of mystery it conveyed."[20] That sense of mystery is fundamental to religious consciousness, as when Henry Vaughan, in his poem cited above, addresses death as "the jewel of the just, / Shining nowhere but in the dark" and comments, "What mysteries do lie beyond thy dust, / Could man outlook that mark."[21]

By ending *Among the Believers* with a poem set on Good Friday, Rash concludes with yet another reference to death, but in this case a death that Christians believe effects humanity's salvation, a death that serves as prelude to resurrection. In "Good Friday, 1995, Driving Westward," Rash's title alludes to John Donne's poem "Good Friday, 1613: Riding Westward," as Fred Chappell may have been the first to point out.[22] Carefully building on images and dates used in the book's first two poems, the poet moves beyond the "seed crop" of death cited in "On the Border" and refers instead to his Baptist ancestors' belief that "the soul is another seed / that endures when flesh and blood are shed, / that all things planted rise toward the sun" (71). Whereas Donne, as Chappell remarks, "projects himself backward in time to observe Christ's crucifixion," "Rash goes forward and envisions Judgment Day."[23] In the poem's final stanza, Rash returns to the term *harvest* to characterize the human pilgrim's passage from life to death and from death to whatever may lie beyond the grave: "I dream them shaking dirt off strange new forms. / Gathered for the last harvest, they hold hands, / take their first dazed steps toward heaven" (71). Thus Rash ends this death-haunted collection with the word *heaven* and with the hope of resurrection. Yet Rash's use of *dream* here emphasizes the visionary nature of this hope, reminding the reader of the crucial "as if" in the poem that concludes part 4: "as if / even the dead were listening."

In his interview with Bjerre, Rash identifies himself as a believer.[24] In comparison to the affirmations of Donne or Vaughan or Flannery O'Connor, however, Rash's are somewhat muted. Although he leaves the reader with a foretaste of resurrection in this Good Friday poem, the book as a whole resonates more with the words that accompany the imposition of ashes on Ash Wednesday: *Remember that you are dust and to dust you shall return.* In Western philosophy and religion, of course, such a recognition of finitude has always been a major means of engaging with ultimate questions about human existence and its relationship to the divine, questions Rash continued to contemplate in his next collection of poems, *Raising the Dead.*

Published the same year as *One Foot in Eden, Raising the Dead,* like that first novel, includes among its main subjects the creation of Lake Jocassee in

upstate South Carolina, a project of the Duke Power Company that led to
the displacement of Jocassee Valley's residents and the removal for reburial
of their interred ancestors before some eight thousand acres were flooded.
In the Cherokee language, the word *Jocassee* means "place of the lost," and
Jocassee is also the name of the legendary daughter of Attakullakulla, the
famed Cherokee chieftain of the late eighteenth century. The flooding of this
valley is Rash's most powerful metaphor of erasure and loss. But *Raising
the Dead* deals only in part with this South Carolina setting. The poems in
three of the book's five parts are set in North Carolina, a fact overlooked by
many of the collection's initial reviewers. Moreover the book's central section
presents poems featuring the poet's cousin, Jeffrey Charles Critcher, who died
in a truck accident at age seventeen and to whose memory Rash dedicates
the book. Born in 1956, just a few years after Rash, Critcher died in 1974,
the year the Jocassee Reservoir reached full capacity. This cousin's death,
Rash has remarked, was the poet's first experience with the death of a near
contemporary.[25]

Raising the Dead is the most tightly structured of Rash's four collections
of poems. Like the four parts of Chappell's *Midquest,* each of the book's five
sections consists of eleven poems, the last of them in each section italicized.
If one adds to that total of fifty-five poems the volume's epigraph from *Henry
IV, Part 1,* the number becomes fifty-six, the year of Critcher's birth. That
epigraph reads as follows:

> Glendower:
> *I can call spirits from the vasty deep.*
> Hotspur:
> *Why, so can I, so can any man.*
> *But will they come when you do call for them?*[26]

Raising the Dead demonstrates Rash's success in invoking those spirits, as
he did with his grandfather's ghost in *Eureka Mill.* While the majority of the
poems here are elegiac and use seven-syllable lines, the book also contains a
villanelle in that form as well as a dramatic monologue, a sonnet variant, and
an epistolary poem in blank verse. The dramatic incidents and diverse characters Rash describes consistently engage the reader's interest. As Peter Campion said in his review of the book in *Poetry,* "A poet who can combine such
lyrical grace with such narrative efficiency deserves our attention."[27] The
reviewer for the Australian journal *Quadrant* went further, claiming, "Here
is the voice that American poetry has been searching for since the deaths of
Frost and Bishop. . . . *Raising the Dead* cannot be praised enough."[28] As in

Among the Believers, most of the poems are a single page or less; only three run longer, the poems' compression intensifying their impact.

The book's first and its final sections focus on events in or near the Jocassee Valley. "Last Service," the opening poem, provides a rapid overview of the desecration wrought by Duke Power. Even after the local church's dead have been disinterred and "Christ's / stained glass face no longer paned / windows," the community still gathers at the site to sing "from memory deep as water / old hymns of resurrection" (3). Because for Rash memory has its own resurrection power, consciousness of the past is crucial, in part to ward off the repetition of preventable losses such as the extinction of species of wildlife. The third poem in part 1 details the killing of "the last panther / ever to stalk Jocassee" (5). "Carolina Parakeet" in part 5 recounts the vanishing of that bird, whose destruction also figures significantly in Rash's novel *The Cove.* This motif recurs in the book's fourth section, too, in "The Wolves at the Asheville Zoo." Rash's work has become increasingly concerned with ecological issues and with human conduct that ravages both nature and other people.

"Under Jocassee," the book's second poem, is reminiscent of "Beneath Keowee" in *Among the Believers,* but the former poem achieves greater immediacy and urgency by beginning with imperative verbs and addressing the reader as *you.* That *you* is urged to take a boat out on Lake Jocassee, to observe the house and barn visible in the water's depths, and then to remember a woman of sixty years past who walks out of that barn, pausing momentarily to gaze skyward. Shifting to indicative present-tense verbs in the poem's closing lines, Rash melds past and present, present and future, showing their interpenetration:

> She believes someone
> has crossed her grave, although
> she will go to her grave,
> a grave you've just passed over,
> wondering why she looked up. (4)

This scene reappears in *One Foot in Eden* and, as indicated in chapter 2, in the short story "Not Waving but Drowning," so its vision of continuity across generations is obviously important to Rash.

Other poems in part 1 likewise emphasize the presence of the past. "The Vanquished," for instance, speaks of the paradoxical lingering absence of Native Americans, their "once-presence / keen as the light of dead stars" (6). In "Shee-Show" that "once-presence" persists in the Cherokee name for the wildflower André Michaux named *shortia galacifolia* but which white settlers came to call Oconee bells (11). Another poem refers to Fort Prince George, the eighteenth-century trading post abandoned by the British in 1768, its remains submerged beneath Lake Keowee after Duke Power dammed the Keowee River, a project completed in 1971. Standing near this site, the poet states, "Inside me / streams blood merging here the night / a captain named Candler wed / Mary Boone" (13). As readers of *The World Made Straight* will recall, a captain named Candler plays a prominent role in that novel and is presumed to have been present at the Shelton Laurel massacre, another example of the interconnections Rash establishes across time and between his poetry and his fiction. The final poem in part 1, "*Deep Water*," reemphasizes the transformation that has occurred in the Jocassee Valley as the poet "*surfaces memory of when / this deep water was a sky*" (14).

Part 5 focuses more narrowly on specific events associated with the formation of the reservoir and the removal of the valley's residents, both living and dead, although the first poem in that section, "Bartram Leaves Jocassee," looks back to naturalist William Bartram's visit to the valley in 1775. Rash details the dismantling of telephone lines; a farmer's preemptive burning of his house and barn before water could inundate them; scarecrows rather than crops standing "like totems" above the slowly rising water, "raised arms spread / like arms of the forsaken" (65); and the dead being exhumed for reburial. But the poet also describes several events after the lake's creation. In "Analepsis," a term that refers to a medicinal restorative or stimulant, he presents a ghost story about "a wailing from deep water" heard by fishermen on the lake (67); "Tremor" similarly alludes to present-day phenomena traceable to the valley's former residents. The title "Death's Harbors" is a metaphor for the now-empty graves that line portions of the lake's floor, while in "Beyond the Dock," the poet witnesses a couple in a boat drop an unknown object into the nighttime water, "in a reservoir so vast / it could bury a valley" (70).

Death and loss and recurring images of water connect the book's three other sections to parts 1 and 5, but the poems in these sections are set in North Carolina, not South Carolina, as noted earlier. "Compass Creek," the first poem in part 2, portrays one of the poet's Welsh ancestors arriving in Buncombe County or Madison County and settling near the French Broad River, his compass situating him in space as the final poem in part 4, "*The Watch*," situates the poet in time as an heir of mortality, the watch of the title having belonged to his deceased maternal grandfather. "Watauga County: 1803," the second poem in part 2, records the deaths of a family trapped in their cabin by a flood, "drowned in the harsh / covenant of that failed ark" (18), while the two repeated lines of the following poem, the villanelle "In Dismal Gorge," are "The lost can stay lost down here" and "Too much too soon disappears" (19). War is one of the major causes of such disappearance throughout Rash's work, as several poems in part 2 also show, three on the Civil War and one on World War II involving the same uncle who appears in *Among the Believers*. The Italian sonnet "Antietam" illustrates continuity across time by juxtaposing the poet's visit to this Civil War battlefield—site of the worst single day's carnage in American history, with some twenty-three thousand casualties—and local lore about vultures returning on each anniversary of the battle, "gathered by some avian memory," the poet imaging them "settling as soft and easy as ashes, / a shuddering quilt of feather and talon" (22). "The Dowry" is an account of continuing postwar animosity between former combatants in Madison County and a tale of grim personal sacrifice to achieve reconciliation, a narrative Rash revised and expanded in his short story of the same title in *Nothing Gold Can Stay*. The dramatic monologue "Black-Eyed Susans" also deals with reconciliation and forgiveness and again illustrates Rash's skillful creation of first-person speakers distinct from himself.

The italicized poem that closes part 2 epitomizes the stoicism that Rash finds integral to the Appalachian worldview. Set at the winter solstice, "*Wolf Laurel*" is a single-sentence tour de force of twenty-six lines telling of a father's death and his three sons' desperate measures to preserve his body from the sheep-killing wolves the men have been pursuing. The poet vividly describes the young men's dilemma:

> . . . *the sons without*
> *lantern, enough lingering light,*
> *know they must leave him or risk*
> *all of them lost, know what waits*
> *for death in that place, so break*
> *a hole in Wolf Laurel's ice,*
> *come back at first light to find*
> *the creek's scab of cold covered*
> *with snow-drift, circling paw prints*
> *brushed away that sons might see*
> *a father's face staring through*
> *the ice as through a mirror.* (29)

In that mirror the sons glimpse their own mortality in yet another of Rash's many memento mori.

At the center of *Raising the Dead* lies Rash's tribute to his deceased cousin and to that cousin's parents, who must confront and withstand their teenaged son's death. The opening poem, "Speckled Trout," credits the cousin with introducing the poet to "those hidden places" where native trout, "bright / shadows of another world," thrive, though the poem ends by foreshadowing the cousin's death through an image of transience: the caught trout's bright colors "already starting to fade" in the poet's hand (33). In these poems Rash's seven-syllable lines might be said to reinforce the theme of mortality by reminding readers of the weekly passage of time through its seven-day cycle. Moreover all eleven of these poems consist of a single stanza, and none runs beyond a page, five of them composed of just one sentence—formal qualities that reflect the brevity of this cousin's life.

Subsequent poems in this section move forward chronologically to and beyond the cousin's death, which is never directly described but instead occurs offstage. Readers see the cousin engaged in farmwork and tempting fate by standing, "when water crests," on a plank bridge that crosses Goshen Creek— even though he has never learned to swim (35). In one intensely ironic poem, "Barn Burning: 1967," the poet depicts his cousin's father's stoic response to the loss of a year's labor when fire destroys the family's tobacco barn:

> A man who gets through a time
> mean as that need not have fears
> of something worse, he would say.
> He said that for seven years. (36)

The irony here turns on the reader's recognition that this man's son dies in 1974.

A similar irony resonates in the following poem, "Work, for the Night Is Coming," a hymn title based on Jesus' words in John 9:4. Here Rash uses a single-sentence poem to imply the energy his cousin invests in finishing topping tobacco plants in an "end row" as darkness falls. The imminence of the cousin's fatal car accident is made explicit in the line "death-clothes scarecrow a bedpost" and in the poem's closing reference to "the future's gold-ripening" as "the harvest / his father will reap alone" (37). Later poems report on the parents' purchase of their son's coffin and the poet's serving as a pallbearer at his cousin's burial, along with family members returning to such activities as hunting and burning off a field.

Among the most poignant poems in part 3 is "At Reid Hartley's Junk-yard," a place the poet and his cousin's mother visit to examine the truck in which the young man died, the father having refused to accompany his wife. Rash describes the junkyard as "this island / reefed with past catastrophes"

(42). At poem's end the mother sits where her son sat at the moment of his death, "her right foot pressed to the brake" (42). This text is followed by the section's concluding italicized poem, *"Spear Point,"* which makes no mention of the cousin but instead recounts the burial of the poet's father, who died in 1978 just four years after the cousin. By shifting to another person's death, Rash stresses the universality of this experience of mortality, an intention reinforced when the spear point itself, found by a kinsman who helps dig this grave, is perceived to be of Native American origin. That spear point, however, might also remind readers of the spear thrust in Jesus' side at his crucifixion. According to Christian theology, on the cross God shares in human suffering and death rather than standing aloof from them. More-over, as St. Paul writes of baptism, "For if we have been united with him in a death like his, we shall certainly be united with him in a resurrection like his" (Romans 6:5 [RSV]).

It is, in fact, to imagery of rebirth that Rash turns in the initial poem in part 4, "The Emerging," in which a young boy survives a tornado by im-mersing himself in a farm pond. Here water is salvific, not destructive. The same is true of fire in "Madison County: June, 1999," a poem reminiscent of those on religious belief in *Among the Believers* and of the short story "Chemistry." In this case the poet recalls a Pentecostal kinsman who "held fire, let it lick / his palm like a pet," a memory that

> . . . still might lead
> me to another state marked
> by no human boundary,
> where my inarticulate
> heart might finally find voice
> in words cured by fire, water. (55)

This poem shares facing pages with "Coke Box," another text of questing, one that owes an obvious debt to Frost's "Directive" in its use of that motif and its reliance on imperatives addressed to the reader.[29] "To get there, fol-low a road / rarely traveled anymore," the poem begins, guiding readers to a remote country store, its "slow emergence like something / brought up from deep water" (54). The reference to deep water recalls earlier poems in which that phrase appears and the movement the book traces from submersion to recovery. The "metal trough" of the Coke box itself, the reader is told, "you open like a coffin," remembering "a man cancer-caught, AWOL / from his death-bed," who had come to this store forty years earlier to have "a cold / sweet longing slaked," a satisfaction available to the reader through memory and the empathetic imagination (54).

Other poems in part 4, such as "The Request" and "Brightleaf," also testify to human triumphs over adversity, the former a one-page condensation of *As I Lay Dying*, minus the self-serving Anse Bundren and Faulkner's grotesquely comic treatment of the circumstances following Addie's death, the latter a celebration of the human impulse to create something of beauty even amid the grimmest of environs. Set in Dismal Gorge ("what sunfall cliff-snagged, leaf-seined," writes the poet in a line indebted to Gerard Manley Hopkins), this poem chronicles a new bride's planting of "hundreds / of dogwoods," her efforts "waking an orchard of light / against that bleak narrative / of place name" (52). In Appalachia the dogwood blossom itself is a symbol of resurrection, of hope and change, and Rash had used it in this way, as chapter 2 noted, in the final story in *The Night the New Jesus Fell to Earth*. Endurance, resourcefulness, courage, fidelity—these are among the virtues Rash attributes to mountain people, virtues that infuse *Raising the Dead* with an aura of hopefulness despite the inundation of the Jocassee Valley. Whether addressing that event in South Carolina or places and events in western North Carolina, Rash invokes universal human experiences and successfully resurrects both his dead kin and the culture that shaped them. Much of the power and appeal of his poetry arises, moreover, from its evocation of "something beyond / what time could fathom," as the first poem in part 5 declares (61).

Although published only two years after *Among the Believers*, *Raising the Dead* represents an artistic advance on the earlier book in its tighter formal structure and in its economy of expression. Rash often achieves such concision by omitting articles—as when he writes of "bullfrogs in pond reeds pausing, / crows voiceless" (47) or when the sons in "*Wolf Laurel*" are "*without / lantern*" (29)—and by omitting possessive pronouns: "sons pressed / hats to hearts like poultices" (50) and "my uncle leaves / bed's-warmth" (40). He continues to use kennings effectively in such terms as *grave-house* for coffin (50) and *fence-thorns* for barbed wire (49), but in this book his thematic focus is sharper as he links past and present, present and absent, with memory the catalyst for his poetic vision. Like the rusted fence-thorns of the poem "Barbed Wire," the events that Rash retrieves from the past are, though "time-dulled, / still able to draw blood" (49).

Nearly a decade passed before the publication of Rash's fourth book of poems, *Waking*. Yet some of the poems that appeared in that book had already been written by the late 1990s. An example is "*Resolution*," which serves as the volume's prefatory poem, one in which, Rash says, "I was attempting to present a sense of my *ars poetica*."[30] For some reason, this poem's title was omitted from the book's table of contents, but Rash clearly views it as crucial to his artistic credo. The poem's multivalent title word has a range of meanings: not only intentionality of purpose or determination but also clarity of vision; not only the separation of something into its constituent parts but also the musical progression from dissonance to consonance; not only the movement from complexity to greater simplicity but also the subsidence of a pathological condition. Other pertinent meanings include the resolving of dramatic tension or conflict in a literary text and the act of solving a problem. "*Resolution*" is brief and so merits quotation in full:

> The surge and clatter of whitewater conceals
> how shallow underneath is, how quickly gone.
> Leave that noise behind. Come here
> where the water is slow and clear.
> Watch the crawfish prance across the sand,
> the mica flash, the sculpen blend with stone.
> It's all beyond your reach though it appears
> as near and known as your outstretched hand.[31]

This initial poem is another bearing the impress of Frost's "Directive" through its imperatives to the reader. Like Emerson and Henry David Thoreau, Rash calls the reader to awareness of the natural world and to consciousness of the limits of human knowledge and power. As Rash noted in an interview with Joyce Brown, one of the two people (along with his uncle Earl Holder) to whom *Waking* is dedicated, "Poetry enlarges the world for us, destroys the illusion that we can grasp it."[32] "*Resolution*" highlights the contrast between appearance and reality and the presumptuousness of the human desire to possess or control nature. The poem directs the reader's attention to water, a natural element essential to life, and the speaker's shift to imperatives and to shorter, more emphatic clauses that form a rhymed couplet in lines 3 and 4 lends the poem a sense of urgency and insists on close examination of specific natural objects: crawfish, sand, mica, sculpen, stone. As the book begins, Rash emphasizes the need for a change in perspective—from the shallows to the depths, from noise to silence, from rapid movement to slower motion, from the superficial and evanescent to the quietly enduring—while at the same time he promotes a stance of humility. "*It's all beyond your reach*," says the speaker, addressing the reader directly, affirming nature's mystery and power. The poem's closing image raises unanswered questions about the aim or intent of that hand. Is it outstretched possessively, graspingly? Or is it extended in welcome, in an effort to embrace rather than seize? Too often that human hand has reached out rapaciously, particularly in Appalachia in extractive industries like coal mining and timbering.

Although "*Resolution*" does not employ seven-syllable lines and instead uses a predominantly iambic meter with lines of varying lengths, all but the first with end rhyme, the majority of the poems in *Waking* do have lines of seven syllables. The book's title term implies the achievement of heightened consciousness to which Thoreau's *Walden* invites readers, with that book's pervasive imagery of sleeping and waking, of dawns as opportunities to begin anew. Given the number of poems here that record deaths of various types, however, readers may also find this title evocative of the vigil maintained after someone has died or something has passed away. In matters of form and literary technique, *Waking* continues the work Rash had done in his preceding two collections, but he has said of this book's poems that "a number of them are more overtly personal than in previous books, childhood moments of transcendence, what Wordsworth called 'spots of time.'"[33] In book 12 of *The Prelude,* Wordsworth writes, "There are in our existence spots of time, / That with distinct pre-eminence retain / A renovating virtue" from which, he adds, "our minds / Are nourished and invisibly repaired."[34] Rash's reference to this passage should alert readers to the poet's indebtedness to the Romantic movement. Indeed one reviewer of *Waking* claimed that "Rash might be his generation's premier Romantic poet."[35]

As in *Among the Believers* and *Raising the Dead,* the poems in *Waking* are divided into five untitled parts. The initial poem in the opening section, "First Memory," records one of the book's Wordsworthian spots of time, what a later poem also calls "moments / unmoored from time" (7). Like "*Resolution*" it runs to just eight lines:

> Dragonflies dip, rise. Their backs
> catch light, purple like church glass.
> Gray barn planks balance on stilts,
> walk toward the pond's deep end.
> A green smell simmers shallows,
> where tadpoles flow like black tears.
> Minnows lengthen their shadows.
> Something unseen stirs the reeds. (3)

As in "*Resolution*" the descriptive detail here features minute particulars in nature, for according to Rash "one of the writer's important functions is to emphasize the natural world."[36] The three-word opening sentence, with its prominent internal rhyme (*flies, rise*), commands attention in a book, like Rash's earlier collections, that includes many single-sentence and two-sentence poems of a full page in length. The farm pond that serves as its setting is a place of mystery, as the final line indicates. But it is also a place of both beauty and ugliness, with intimations of sadness in the simile "like black tears." Verbs of action energize the poem, in which even the inanimate barn planks "balance" and "walk," and "smell simmers." The poem's relatively simple syntax bespeaks a child's perspective, and the large number of stressed syllables in each line mirrors the child's excitement, a point made by Robert West, who comments: "The ratio of stressed to unstressed syllables is extraordinarily high, so that the poem sounds relentlessly emphatic. It's an ingenious effect for a poem about the world making its first deep impression on a child."[37] The depth of that impression is reinforced by Rash's decision to use present tense in "First Memory," a choice that underscores the persistence of the past, its ongoing impact in the here and now.

"First Memory" grounds the child-poet in the natural world, although a natural scene into which human artifacts have already intruded—in this instance the plank dock. For Rash, as for many Appalachian poets, nature is generally presented not apart from human activity but as part of a dynamic interaction based on an agrarian lifestyle (or on memories of that lifestyle). Thus in the second poem in part 1, "The Trout in the Springhouse," Rash recalls his relatives' use of a trout to gauge the purity of their water supply. The trout has a role to play on the family farm, a setting also depicted in the following poem, "Milking Traces." In fact Rash often employs agrarian settings in *Waking*. The word *barn* appears in more than a fifth of the book's poems, and farmwork, fields, lofts, and other farming-related sites and activities are mentioned in at least a dozen additional poems.

Yet Rash is no sentimental, nostalgic agrarian, as several of the poems in parts 2 and 3 reveal, for he never minimizes the hardships of farming or the vagaries of nature, with its frequent indifference to the farmer's well-being. In many of these poems, nature is antagonist rather than ally. The kinsman of whom the poet writes in "Spillcorn," for example, turns from farming to logging because he is "a man needing steady work / no hailstorm or August drought / could take away" (23). The farmwife in "Mirror" purchases that object "after five years of breaking / land that had tried to break her" (25), while another farmwife (in "Woman Among Lightning: Catawba County Fair, 1962") chooses to ride out a thunderstorm on a Ferris wheel instead of seeking safety:

> leaving the ground where her days
> are measured in rows, the hoe
> swinging like a metronome

> while life leaks away like blood
> on land always wanting more,
> wanting more, . . . (27)

Part 3 of *Waking* seems intended to reinforce the antinostalgic stance of
the poems just quoted. That section's second poem, "The Reaping," tells of
a father's discovery of his dead son after an accident involving a hay baler.
The third poem in part 3, "Dismal," speaks of this place-name's origin:

> from years of breaking hoes and backs
> against a leached-out, angled ground,
> that grudgingly gave up each rock,
> yet freed like Bible plagues the nests
> of yellow jackets, rattlesnakes. (34)

In the following poem, "Hearth," a blizzard forces an elderly man to burn,
"oak plank by oak plank," his cabin's porch and back room to keep himself
alive (35). And in "Tobacco" the first-person plural speakers lament the
hardships and disillusionment that raising this crop produces: "Good harvest
or bad we sank deeper in debt" (37).

This section concludes with a dramatic monologue, "Three A.M. and the
Stars Were Out," spoken by an elderly veterinarian who describes the assorted misfortunes of his occupation: "I know more likely than not / I'll be
arriving too late, / what's to be done best done with / rifle or shotgun" (44).
Yet this old vet relishes "what stays unseen except on / country roads after
midnight" and recalls with pleasure those nights when everything works out
successfully, when he enjoys "watching stars / awake in their wide pasture"
in the poem's striking closing image (44–45). Through personification and
this metaphor of the heavens as a pasture, Rash has his speaker animate and
domesticate the stars. Instead of the frightening abysses of space into which
Pascal gazes in his *Pensées* or the "high cold star" Stephen Crane invokes
to illustrate nature's indifference to human well-being in "The Open Boat,"
Rash's image establishes a continuity with nature like that in Emerson's
essay *Nature*, though Emerson presents the stars as emblems of the sublime,
whereas Rash's term *pasture* transforms the stars into farmyard animals.
This metaphor enables Rash to conclude part 3 on a positive note despite his
many negative depictions of nature's impact on human beings.

Having demonstrated his unsentimental attitude toward nature and toward agrarian living, Rash devotes many of the poems in the book's final
section to a lyric celebration of nature's beauty and benefits, focusing on an
intimate connection between human beings and the natural world. In the

opening poem of Part 5, for instance, "Reading the Leaves," as in the earlier "Spillcorn," his diction and figurative language interweave nature and literary culture, agriculture and the cultivation of the mind and imagination, when an uncle scrutinizes his tobacco crop for blue mold and cutworms, "follow[ing] / the long sentences of each row" (63). The tobacco barn's tin roof resembles, Rash writes, "a facedown book" beneath which the tobacco leaves, bound to the rafters, are "brittle pages," pages "strung together as Celts once / strung leaves on cords to compose / the first words of Albion" (63). The final line here illustrates the antiquity of this link between human beings and nature, an interaction that educates, that illuminates. This imagery portraying nature as language is reminiscent of Emerson and other American and British Romantics, and such imagery also appears in Rash's earlier poem about the kinsman turned logger, a man who spends his lunch break reading a book carried into the gorge where he is engaged in timbering:

> what had roughed his hands now smooth
> as his fingertips turned
> the leaves, each word whispered soft
> as the wind reading the trees. (23)

The closing lines of both these poems draw not only on Emerson but also on Walt Whitman's unifying metaphor in *Leaves of Grass*.

Like Emerson and Whitman and his fellow Appalachian poet Robert Morgan, Rash underscores the textuality of nature. In "Waterdogs," which describes a season of drought, he refers to people for whom "clouds are spread out scrolls written / in a lost tongue," people unlike, he says, those farmers attuned to nature for whom "passing clouds read / like pages turned in a book," men able to discern what Rash calls the "damasked commas" that are the natural phenomena of the poem's title, clouds promising rain (64). Similarly in "Watauga County: 1962," a poem about the pleasures of blackberrying, Rash begins by noting the "smell of honeysuckle bright / as dew beads stringing lines on / the writing spider's silk page" (68). The synesthetic merging of smell and sight in these lines attests to the plenitude evident in nature, as does the poem's penultimate line, "the sweet wine of blackberry," which the speaker raises to his mouth in eating the picked berries, this wine image seeming to confirm his communion with nature (68). Just a few pages later, in "Raspberries," the poet compares those berries, "dangling in dew-light," to "ruby thimbles" and praises the sweetness, the "warm / slow savor," stored up by canning the berries (71). In this poem Rash's high valuation of nature is apparent in his choice of the terms *ruby* and *rubies*.

Among the most prominent images of nature's beauty in part 5 is that of dew, which appears not only in all three of the poems just cited but in six of the twelve poems in this final section. Rather than using dew to suggest the evanescence of nature's creatures, including human beings, Rash focuses on other traits that can be associated with dew: darkness and cold in two instances but more often scintillating light, as when in "Boy in a Boxcar" he envisions the poem's speaker as "watch[ing] from trapped dark the sun wake / grass-stars harbored in dew beads" (66). It is the radiance and beauty of nature that the poet highlights in these words, as he does in the book's final image of a stringer of fish—"bluegills, browns, and rainbows"—pulled from the water of Price Lake in Watauga County:

> I remember
> how it surfaced glistening
> like a crystal chandelier,
> the fish shimmering color
> as if raised in prism-light. (74)

In this passage, which concludes the book, Rash's diction and figurative language once again interweave natural and man-made objects. The caught fish, presumably, will nourish the speaker's family, as nature also nourishes in the poems about blackberries and raspberries.

Waking presents nature itself in prism-light, illuminating its multiple facets. The closer examination of nature called for in "*Resolution*" is not always reassuring, however, for even the sculpen of that poem prove to be spiny junk fish, not the colorful, edible rainbows and bluegills of "Price Lake." Rash portrays nature as both destructive and nurturing, threatening and sustaining. But as Emily Dickinson does in her serenely dualistic response to nature in her poem that begins "Without a smile—Without a Throe, / A Summer's soft Assemblies go," a poem that she concludes by labeling nature "a dissembling Friend,"[38] so Rash in *Waking* ultimately views nature as a potential friend, however unpredictable, whose benefits human beings must cherish and preserve, as novels such as *Saints at the River* and *Serena* likewise indicate.

In addition to this collection's important focus on nature, *Waking* also incorporates a wide array of human characters and of object poems such as "Junk Car in Snow," "Pocketknives," "Car Tags," and "The Belt." "The Wallet" reprises the situation related in Rash's short story "My Father Like a River," revealing the autobiographical source that underlies that text. "Bonding Fire," the first poem in part 2, draws on a passage in *Saints at the River*, as does "The Girl in the River," while the fish tale in "Muskellunge" anticipates the one told in "Their Ancient, Glittering Eyes," the first story in *Chemistry*. "Resonance" and "Rhiannon" both allude to the Welsh tales collected in *The Mabinogion,* as do at least two of the poems in *Among the Believers,* and the title "Good Friday, 2006: Shelton Laurel" links this poem not only to others about that Civil War massacre but also to the final poem in *Among the Believers,* also set on Good Friday. Familiar place-names likewise abound: not just Shelton Laurel, Watauga County, and Madison County but also Dismal Mountain, Boone, Blowing Rock, Marshall, Middlefork Creek, and Goshen Creek. Such self-referential intertextuality does not leave the impression of tired repetition or limited subject matter but rather of abundant creative resources deployed by a fully realized artistic vision. "My goal has always been," Rash has stated, "for the poems, stories, and novels to inform and enrich one another."[39]

Rash's skills as a poet should place him in the front ranks of contemporary American poets, but he has yet to achieve the recognition he deserves in this genre, at least if one takes note of his omission from such anthologies as *The Oxford Book of American Poetry* (2006) and *The Penguin Anthology of Twentieth-Century American Poetry* (2011). The small presses with which he has published his poetry have lacked the financial resources to market those books effectively despite the admiring reviews they have received. It will likely take a volume of collected poems or of new and selected poems to overcome the relative obscurity his remarkable poetry has tended to experience outside the American South.

CHAPTER 4

One Foot in Eden, Saints at the River, and The World Made Straight

Despite the positive reviews Rash's first five books of short stories and poetry received, it was not until his first novel, *One Foot in Eden,* appeared that he began to garner wider national recognition. Published in 2002, this novel was a "breakout book" for Rash. As he told interviewer Robert Birnbaum, "It got reviewed in places I had never been reviewed," including the *Los Angeles Times,* which offered high praise, characterizing the novel as "equal parts vintage crime novel and southern gothic," "a veritable garden of earthly disquiet."[1] Asked by another interviewer if he had been apprehensive about attempting a different genre, Rash replied, "Very much so. Because I'd tried a few novels before and I'd never had any success, and I was fearful of that kind of [time] commitment."[2] Rash worked on this book four years, the manuscript winning the Novello Literary Award sponsored by the Public Library of Charlotte and Mecklenburg County, North Carolina. *One Foot in Eden* was published by the Novello Festival Press rather than a major commercial publisher, although Rash has said that "a noted publisher" had expressed interest in the book but wanted him to revise the manuscript to limit its narration to a single point of view, a change Rash wisely refused to make.[3] By creating five distinctive first-person narrators, he not only demonstrates his skill with characterization and vernacular language but also reinforces the book's moral and thematic complexity while evoking the incremental repetition readers find in an epic such as Homer's *Odyssey.*

According to Rash, his novels originate not with a theme, setting, or event but with an image: "I don't plot out my novels and I don't outline them. . . . I just start with that image."[4] For *One Foot in Eden,* that originating image was "a man standing in his field, his crops dying around him."[5]

Rash first wrought that image into a poem, then tried it as a short story, before developing it into a novel, the genre he says that he finds most difficult: "There are days when I'm writing novels where I'd rather just stick the pencils right in my eyeballs than try to write another sentence."[6] Like the poems of the opening and closing sections of *Raising the Dead, One Foot in Eden* is set in the Jocassee Valley, and its characters know that their farmland will eventually be submerged by the hydroelectric project planned by Carolina Power (as Duke Power is named in this book). Though that project will not be completed for nearly twenty years, Rash keeps the reader aware of its inevitable consequences through the water imagery that pervades the novel. The threat of erasure haunts these characters, as it haunts Rash in terms of the disappearance of this area's agrarian lifestyle and of Appalachia's history and cultural traditions, an erasure manifest in the recurring appropriation of Appalachians' private property for national parks and commercial uses. The novel opens in 1952, some fifty years before its publication date, thus reflecting Rash's consciousness of the past and its ongoing impact, one of the major themes of not only his work but also that of southern writers generally, including many authors from Appalachia. As Rash states, "That backward look is an important dimension of Appalachian writing because it demonstrates a sense of history, a sense that what has happened before may happen again. We have a country which needs that lesson right now, a sense of history."[7] Such historical consciousness is particularly evident in the novel's initial narrator, Sheriff Will Alexander.

The book's title, however, through its reference to Eden, moves beyond history to archetype and myth, and it therefore invites moral and religious interpretations of the book. As the novel's epigraph reveals, Rash's title is taken from a poem of the same name by twentieth-century Scottish poet Edwin Muir, which also provided the title of Muir's last published collection (1956). The epigraph quotes the first five lines of that poem, which uses agrarian imagery appropriate to the novel and emphasizes the inextricable interweaving of the "crops of love and hate" human beings have sown.[8] Muir's poem goes on to say, "Time's handiworks by time are haunted, / And nothing now can separate / The corn and tares compactly grown," lines that seem especially pertinent to the moral status of Billy and Amy Holcombe in Rash's novel. Yet the fact that the poem's speaker still has a foot in Eden suggests the duality—or multiplicity—of human identity, its innocence as well as guilt, and the persistence of visions of paradise amid a fallen world. Moreover Muir's poem presents a version of what theologians call the Fortunate Fall, *felix culpa:* "But famished field and blackened tree / Bear flowers in Eden never known." Among those flowers Muir lists "hope and faith and pity and love," virtues evident in the characters of Rash's novel, and he concludes his poem with the following couplet: "Strange blessings never in paradise / Fall from these beclouded skies," the final line stressing the word *Fall* by abridging its initial foot.[9] Whether or not Rash endorses the idea of a Fortunate Fall, he clearly embraces Muir's concept of the admixture of good and evil in human nature and his notion of blessings arising amid and despite the presence of evil.

Rash has said of this first novel, "In a way *One Foot in Eden* is my *Crime and Punishment*," a comment that also invites readers to consider the book's moral and religious implications.[10] Like Fyodor Dostoyevsky's novel, Rash's revolves around a murder and the consequences of that killing, its psychological and spiritual impact on the perpetrators of the crime and their son, who eventually discovers that the victim was his biological father. Rash does not write a traditional whodunit, however, because the reader learns almost immediately who has committed the murder; instead he focuses on the circumstances and consequences of that act. The story is told in separately titled sections by five first-person narrators: "the High Sheriff" (Will Alexander), "the Wife" (Amy Holcombe), "the Husband" (Billy Holcombe), "the Son" (Isaac), and "the Deputy" (Bobby Murphree). The murder victim is Holland Winchester, from whom Rash distances readers by not assigning Holland a section to narrate.

The action begins two weeks before Holland's death, when the sheriff and his deputy are called to intervene in a brawl at a honky-tonk called the Borderline, a name indicative of the liminal spaces so prominent in Rash's work and likewise suggestive of the fluid intermingling of good and evil in Muir's poem. Holland, a disaffected Korean War veteran who wears a leather pouch containing eight dried-up ears from enemy soldiers, has initiated the violence at the Borderline. "It was as close to war as I'd seen since the Pacific," says the sheriff, himself a veteran of World War II who fought at Guadalcanal but whose war souvenirs are a sword and a rifle, not cropped ears (4). When Holland asks the sheriff, "You reckon them ears can still hear?" Alexander responds, "The dead don't hear and they don't speak. . . . They just disappear"—words that prove both prophetic in terms of Holland's corpse's disappearance and ironic insofar as the dead Holland does, in fact, continue to affect others' lives (6). His murder takes place in the heat of August during a drought, an emblem of the infertility that also affects such characters as Billy and the sheriff's wife, Janice.

One of the aims of Rash's work has always been to subvert stereotypes of Appalachia and its people, stereotypes that assume Appalachians are lazy, stupid, illiterate or minimally educated, violent, impoverished, and incestuous.[11] His portrait of Sheriff Alexander illustrates some of the ways he combats such prejudices, for Alexander has completed three years at Clemson University and continues to educate himself by extensive reading in history. He alludes to *Hamlet* (though that allusion escapes his deputy) and shows himself to be a sensitive, caring person (4). Although his ancestors have farmed the Jocassee Valley for nearly two hundred years, the sheriff has left farming for law enforcement, moving into the town of Seneca and thus becoming estranged from his father and brother. His marriage is also troubled—his wife, a town girl and doctor's daughter, disapproving of his "hillbilly" ways (7).

By opening the novel with Alexander as narrator, Rash imbues the book with a historical and philosophical resonance unavailable through the perspectives of Amy, Billy, or the teenaged Isaac. The sheriff's given name, Will, reinforces issues of choice and conscious intention versus matters of accident, chance, or fate that recur throughout this initial section—indeed throughout the novel. The sheriff acknowledges, for instance, the heavy toll that "bad luck," including Billy's bout with polio, has taken on the Holcombes over generations (14). Alexander himself left Clemson after three years following a knee injury inflicted by a teammate during a football scrimmage, "an accident" (34). Janice's father's financial reversals in the stock market crash of 1929 exacerbated the couple's difficulties following the loss of Alexander's football scholarship, causing Will to drop out of college to work at the ironically named Liberty Mill. Yet while this football injury certainly altered his life, the sheriff ultimately attributes his current situation to the choices he has made. He also believes that Amy Holcombe has made a choice between Holland and Billy, choosing Billy and accepting responsibility for that choice. At times, too, the sheriff seems to voice concerns central to Rash's literary project, as when he emphasizes William Bartram's roles as both historian and naturalist, roles Rash also assumes: "He [Bartram] understood that things disappeared. . . . He wanted to get it all down. He wanted things to be remembered" (51). These words ring as true for Rash as for Bartram, as does the Augustinian restlessness to which the sheriff seems to allude in speaking of Hank Williams's singing of "the high lonesome": "It was a kind of yearning, a sense that part of your heart was unfilled. A preacher would say it was man's condition since leaving Eden" (48–49). Such yearning also characterizes the narrator's father in Rash's short story "Chemistry."

Although the sheriff rightly suspects Billy of murdering Holland, as does Holland's mother, who is aware of her son's affair with Amy and hears a shot from the adjacent Holcombe farm on the day her son disappears, Alexander underestimates Billy's intelligence and is unable to locate Holland's body. As a result, at the end of his section, the sheriff can only say to Holcombe, who is making a crib for Amy's unborn child, "You got away with it," words that subsequent events prove to be deeply ironic (57). Yet the rain that falls at the end of this section suggests that the summer's drought has ended, that regeneration is imminent.

The novel's second section is narrated by Amy, who provides background information about her pregnancy and Holland's murder and advances the plot by moving forward in time through Isaac's birth and its aftermath. Whereas the sheriff's section focuses primarily on the search for Holland's body during the two days immediately after he vanishes, Amy's narration encompasses a more extended period of time, more than a year, as readers learn of the visit to the doctor that confirmed Billy's sterility in December 1951; Amy's brief affair with Holland to conceive a child in April 1952, an affair she ends as soon as she becomes pregnant; Holland's death in August; and Isaac's birth in January 1953. In both sections Rash's skillful handling of flashbacks and memories enlarges the temporal focus beyond these principal events.

Despite the adultery Amy commits and the murder her actions precipitate, Rash makes her a sympathetic character. As the opening pages of her section indicate, her intense desire for a child results from the community's definition of female identity in terms of marriage and motherhood—a definition enforced by the women whom Amy encounters. Her love for Billy is deep and sincere, and except for the couple's failure to produce a child, their marriage has been happy. Desperate to conceive, Amy goes to visit the Widow Glendower, a midwife and herbal healer reputed by some to be a witch. The widow's name links her to the Glendower of Rash's epigraph to *Raising the Dead,* who claims, in Shakespeare's *Henry IV, Part 1,* "I can call spirits from the vasty deep," and who in the play also declares, "Why, I can teach you . . . to command the devil."[12] This character also derives from Appalachian folklore, as does Nora Bonesteel in Sharyn McCrumb's ballad novels, gifted with "the sight" and other seemingly supernatural powers.[13] Sheriff Alexander had visited her in the book's opening section, on his father's advice, in hopes of obtaining information that would help him locate Holland's body, a visit Rash includes to forestall the reader's assumption that Amy is simply superstitious. Amy, in fact, visits the Widow three times: once to seek remedies for Billy's sterility, once more when those remedies fail, and yet again when Billy falls seriously ill before and after Isaac's birth. It is the Widow, during that second visit, who proposes that Amy "lay down" with her neighbor Holland to conceive (77). These treks to the Widow's remote cabin, particularly the third, made at night in a February snowstorm, endow Amy with heroic qualities, evoking the classical journey motif. For the assistance the Widow renders during Amy's first two visits, she refuses Amy's proffered payment, asking only that she serve as midwife when the baby is born—a request that Amy later ignores. But on the third occasion, the Widow accepts the Gold Star that Holland offered Amy for the unborn child when he recognized Amy had become pregnant, a medal he received for gallantry in action. That Gold Star will subsequently provide evidence of Billy's and Amy's roles in Holland's death once the Widow delivers it to Holland's mother—this act motivated, seemingly, by revenge for Amy's broken promise.

Rash's intricate plotting of the novel's action maintains suspense throughout, for although Amy sees Billy shoot Holland, her husband does not explain how he disposes of Holland's body. Not till part 3, narrated by Billy, does the reader learn how that corpse has been concealed from Sheriff Alexander and his search party: Billy binds it with barbed wire to the upper limb of an oak tree, killing his beloved workhorse, Sam (Billy claims it broke its leg), beneath the tree to account for the vultures that will gather there. Rash has said that he wrote Billy's section first,[14] but by placing it at the center of the book's five parts, he underscores Billy's assumption of responsibility for what has happened. This stance aligns him psychologically with the sheriff, a connection Rash also emphasizes by making them cousins and by giving both men limps, their physical disability, like Joy-Hulga's wooden leg in Flannery O'Connor's "Good Country People," indicative of moral and spiritual flaws.

As with Amy, Rash insures that Billy remains a sympathetic character despite his murder of Holland. A victim of polio as a child, a disease to which he attributes his sterility, Billy is hard working, having bought twenty acres of land from Holland's father after growing up in a sharecropping household. He loves Amy and fears losing her when he becomes aware of her affair with Holland, especially since Billy was a schoolmate of the rebellious and violent Holland and knows Amy is wrong to assume that her words of rejection will keep Holland away from her. The murder is made more ambiguous when Holland holds the barrel of Billy's shotgun against his own chest, taunting Billy and insisting, "Settle it now one way or another, Holcombe" (126). While Holland proclaims, "What's swelling her belly is mine, not yours," Amy had earlier told her husband, "It's my child, Billy. But it can be ours if you want" (125, 118). Billy is no cold-hearted killer, for following his concealing of Holland's body, he prays for his victim and asks Holland and God for forgiveness, though he acknowledges, "it was a sorry excuse for a prayer, asking nothing more of me than some muttered words" (137). Billy recognizes that authentic spirituality makes demands on people. The following evening, after he begins working on a crib for the unborn baby, he again prays for forgiveness, remembering "the sinner on the cross Jesus had saved" and vowing to be "a good daddy" to the child (154).

That commitment intensifies in the closing pages of Billy's section following his return to the oak in November to bury Holland's remains, a process during which he recalls a passage he attributes to the Gospel of Mark, "about the sins of the father being laid on the child," a prospect from which he longs to protect the child, as Amy does when she chooses the name Isaac, "a Godly name . . . [to] put him in God's favor" (156, 104). Billy never doubts that God's judgment awaits him. Falling ill the day after he buries Holland's bones, he nearly dies but is eventually cured by the willow bark and boneset tea whose ingredients Widow Glendower gives Amy in section 2. When Billy sees the baby for the first time in a month, he notes that "Holland Winchester's dark eyes stared straight into mine. . . . It was like those eyes was God's hands opening palm up" (158). Instead of choosing what he considers "the easy thing to do"—turning himself in—Billy elects "to do right by Holland," to "give his child shoes and a full belly and teach him how to be a man." "To do those things," he adds, "I'd have to . . . love him for what he was—a son." For Rash this stance is not a rationalization but a moral commitment, one reinforced by Billy's concluding words in section 3: "I hadn't got away with nothing" (159).

One of the major literary achievements of this novel is Rash's skillful use of vernacular language appropriate to the Appalachian region and to his characters. In creating that language, he drew upon the talk he had heard as a child during summers on his grandmother's farm near Boone.[15] At the same time, he sought to avoid "evoking Snuffy Smith" and other stereotypes that demean Appalachians: "Thus, in *Eden*, I de-emphasized non-standard grammar and avoided contractions."[16] Instead, he says, "I emphasized distinctively Appalachian words, and most of all a cadence true to the Appalachian speech I heard while growing up."[17] Because Sheriff Alexander has been exposed to higher education at Clemson, his section contains much less regional dialect than Amy's and Billy's, though the sheriff does at times use such locutions in his dialogue and, less frequently, at some points in his narration, as when he speaks of "a bad habit I couldn't get shed of" (3) or refers to having "a look-see" (7) or mentions "blue holes" in the river as likely hiding places for Holland's body (54).

It is in Amy's and Billy's sections that Rash's artistry with vernacular speech is most evident and where it is combined with a profusion of figurative language consistent with the characters' experiences and situations in life. As Rash explains, "I use a lot of similes in my vernacular because I feel it's a way of showing the creativity and the intelligence of the character. They may not use an educated language, but there's a beauty and poetry and inventiveness in their language."[18] Here again Rash undercuts stereotypes of

Appalachians as unintelligent. Among the distinctively Appalachian words Rash uses in Amy's section are "glimsen" for a glimpse or glance (85), "yarbing" for gathering herbs (74), "grabbled" (105), "play-pretty" (73), and "noon-dinner" for lunch (65). Amy often shifts the customary part of speech in which a word is employed in Standard English, as when she remarks that "rocks big as haystacks skinnied the trail" (68) or says the sheriff's presence "didn't heavy my mind much as it ought have" (96), the compression of the latter statement also reflective of Appalachian vernacular. Amy's section is rife with such language, including many similes drawn from nature, as when the midwife who delivers Isaac moves her hand on Amy's stomach "like she was feeling a pumpkin to certain it was ripe" (100). She also uses the "might could" phrasing of Appalachian dialect and regularly substitutes of for have in verb constructions.

Billy's section is even richer in such vernacular usage. The first half-dozen pages of that section include words such as "quiles" for coils (115), "slaunchways" for aslant (116), "swaged" for assuaged (118), the phrase "come shackling" (115), and both "suspicioned" (116) and "confidenced" (120) used as verbs. Later Billy uses "scawmy," a word that also appears in Rash's poetry, to indicate a damp, foggy day (155). Despite Rash's claim that he minimized nonstandard grammar in this novel, Billy's section contains many instances of subject-verb errors, double negatives, and errors involving irregular verbs, as in the sentence, "I'd of went yesterday" (127). Rather than detracting from the book, such language lends the novel authenticity because Billy's section is likewise filled with vividly detailed similes. For instance Rash has him observe how "the air laid on the night still and stale as stump water" (119) and describe his dry throat as "parched as roasted chestnuts" (120). After one occasion when Amy and Holland make love, Billy sees "a spot on her neck purpled like a fox grape," and he refers to a drought-stricken dogwood Amy has planted as "no more alive than a iron stob," the dropped n of an before a vowel sound another characteristic of Appalachian dialect (116, 122). Rash's meticulous re-creation of that dialect gives the novel much of its appeal.

That vernacular is largely absent from Isaac's section, however, perhaps because that section is set nearly twenty years after Holland's death, in the fall of 1970, as Isaac approaches his eighteenth birthday, by which time popular culture and public education had reduced the persistence of that dialect among a younger generation. Whatever the explanation, the absence of that language makes the more modern era represented by Isaac seem colorless in comparison, as Rash's focus becomes Isaac's discovery of his presumed parents' complicity in his biological father's death, a revelation made to the young man by Holland's mother, who had befriended Isaac years earlier, knowing that he was her grandson. With the Jocassee Valley beginning to disappear beneath the hydroelectric project's rising waters, Mrs. Winchester insists that Isaac confront Billy and Amy so that Holland's remains can receive a proper burial, and she gives Isaac the Gold Star to elicit a confession from the Holcombes.

By this point in the novel, the Holcombes have moved to Seneca, where Billy is employed in a mill, his farm soon to be submerged. The nearby mountains have been clear-cut, one of many scenes of environmental destruction in Rash's work. In fact an employee of Carolina Power informs Isaac callously, "Every last one of you hillbillies is going to be flushed out of this valley like shit down a commode" (184). Sheriff Alexander is forced to evict his own brother from the family farm, while Mrs. Winchester faces being moved to a nursing home. Instead, like the farmer in "A Homestead on the Horsepasture" in *Raising the Dead*, she drenches her home in kerosene and sets it ablaze, though unlike that farmer, she chooses to die in the flames, "like those monks in Vietnam I'd seen on TV," says Isaac, who pulls her charred body from the burning house on the same day she reveals that Holland, not Billy, is his father (177).

This section's main temporal focus is the two-day period during which, first, that revelation occurs and then the Holcombes, accompanied by Sheriff Alexander, retrieve Holland's remains. The latter episode takes place as heavy rains fall, causing the river the four characters must cross to grow dangerous, especially for Billy, who has never learned to swim. Although the sheriff urges the Holcombes to let the rising water cover up the past, Billy and Amy want Holland properly buried. When Alexander tells Isaac that unless Isaac leaves Holland's remains on the far side of the river Deputy Murphree will have to proceed with a murder charge, Isaac realizes that "I had to make a choice between the man who'd raised me or the sack of bones and dirt in my hand" (198). Despite the emotional turmoil into which Mrs. Winchester's revelations have plunged him, particularly regarding his feelings about Billy, Isaac recognizes that "my not being his son hadn't stopped him from loving me like a son" (196). Adding the Gold Star to the bag, Isaac lets the sack slip into the river. "Let the dead bury the dead," intones the sheriff, echoing Jesus' words in Luke 9:60 (198). Isaac's section shows all three Holcombes, as well as Sheriff Alexander, making choices based on acceptance of moral responsibility and, in the case of the sheriff and Isaac, reaching decisions determined not by strictly legal concerns but by the virtues of mercy and love. Because Billy and Amy drown while attempting to return across the river, the novel bears the imprint of a tragic sensibility, its author seeming to imply that willingness to make amends does not always exempt someone from the dire consequences of earlier actions.

Isaac, however, survives, as Deputy Bobby Murphree's brief closing section, more coda than climax, reports. Bobby sees the Jocassee Valley's dead disinterred for reburial in a scene reminiscent of the final poem in *Raising the Dead*. But six months later a coffin overlooked in that process appears in Lake Jocassee, a coffin Bobby realizes is that of Widow Glendower. Intensely superstitious, he sinks the Widow's remains in the lake's depths, then puts salt in the coffin to ward off witchcraft and secures the lid for the coffin's reburial. It is Bobby who is given the novel's closing words: "This was a place for the lost," the last four words in that sentence translating the Cherokee term *Jocassee* (214). Amid that place for the lost, however, Rash creates a tale of enduring love and of good outweighing evil. The climactic scene in Isaac's section—the recovery and ultimate disposition of Holland's remains— evokes the "hope and faith and pity and love" that Muir's poem affirms. At the same time, Rash's return to the Widow at novel's end seems meant to reflect the complexity of the human condition, its profound intermingling of good and evil, joy and sorrow, for although the Widow is more healer than destroyer, she remains a morally ambiguous figure, her motive for giving Holland's medal to Mrs. Winchester never explained. She thus exemplifies the moral duality of human nature. But Rash makes it clear that the flooding of this valley cannot be seen as a sign of divine judgment, like Noah's flood, but is solely a consequence of human decision-making, of choices that harm all the valley's inhabitants, human and nonhuman. The Jocassee Valley's submersion becomes a metaphor for the erasure of Appalachian culture—and, by extension, for the marginalization or erasure of any smaller segment of a larger, more powerful group or nation.

Like *One Foot in Eden, Saints at the River* (2004) is set in Oconee County, South Carolina. But unlike events in Rash's first novel and all his subsequent ones through *The Cove*, the action of *Saints* occurs not in an earlier time period but in a present time almost contemporaneous with the date of the novel's publication. Yet through the experiences two of the characters have had in Biafra, Rwanda, and Kosovo, the book incorporates the consciousness of history—in this case of genocidal atrocities—typical of Rash's work. Rash has said of this book, "I wanted to write a novel about environmental issues, but one that refused simplifications. I picked a situation where I was essentially in conflict with myself, the part of me who is an environmentalist and the part of me who is a parent."[19] This book's originating image, Rash explains, was that of a drowned child's face "staring up at him through water," an image that also appears in his poem "The Girl in the River" in *Waking* and in the short story "Something Rich and Strange" in *Nothing Gold Can Stay.*[20] In the novel twelve-year-old Ruth Kowalsky is that drowning victim, her death described in the book's italicized opening section. Ruth's body is trapped in a hydraulic, and the attempt to recover it precipitates the conflict between her parents and a group of environmentalists led by Luke Miller. While Rash sets this drowning on a fictional river he calls the Tamassee, he has acknowledged that a similar drowning occurred on the Chattooga River in upstate South Carolina and that a portable dam was installed there, as in the novel, in an effort to retrieve the victim's body.[21] As in *One Foot in Eden* and in many of Rash's poems and short stories, water imagery is integral to this book.

Rash links these first two novels not just by setting both in Oconee County but also by mentioning such specific place-names as Licklog Mountain (where Billy Holcombe buries Holland Winchester's remains) and by referring to the Winchester family as having resided in the area for two hundred years. The surnames Watson and Lusk and Alexander appear in both books, and readers learn that *Saints*'s narrator's maternal grandfather was a Holcombe. Moreover one of the characters in *Saints* was born in Chester, South Carolina, a detail that ties this novel to *Eureka Mill* as well. Such interconnections are a major feature of Rash's writing as he depicts Appalachian South Carolina and North Carolina over two centuries and more.

In contrast to his first novel, which had five first-person narrators, *Saints* has just one, Maggie Glenn, a twenty-eight-year-old native of Oconee County now working as a photojournalist in the state capital, Columbia. Maggie and her coworker, reporter Allen Hemphill, whose book on Rwanda was a finalist for the Pulitzer Prize, are assigned to cover the intensifying conflict that arises from Ruth's drowning. At this point the girl's body has already been trapped in the river for three weeks, with most of the novel's action focused on the two-week period that follows. Because the Tamassee is protected by the federal Wild and Scenic Rivers Act of 1978, Ruth's father encounters strong opposition to his plan to have a portable dam temporarily installed on the river. As Luke knows, developers of property along the river would love to have a precedent established that allowed for its alteration. Local residents are ambivalent about the recovery efforts but want to have their long-term experience with the river consulted and respected by outsiders such as the Kowalskys and the engineer who owns the portable dam company, all of them Midwesterners. Maggie's loyalties are complicated by the fact that nearly ten years earlier she not only was among Luke's followers but also was his lover. Allen, on the other hand, aligns himself with the Kowalskys because he lost his own daughter, along with his wife, in an auto accident. Maggie's return to Oconee County is further complicated by her estrangement from her dying father, whom she continues to hold responsible for a childhood accident that left her brother Ben's face horribly scarred by scalding water and that burned Maggie herself, though much less seriously. The first and last word of chapter 1 is *Ghosts,* a signal that the past still haunts Maggie, as it does Allen and, to a lesser extent, Luke.

In tracing the novel's principal conflicts, Rash resists didacticism by carefully balancing the characters' competing views and by portraying all the characters as flawed in some way. Mr. Kowalsky is a grieving parent whose loss evokes sympathy, but he is also arrogant and condescending toward the local folk, whom he addresses as "you hillbillies."[22] Luke speaks movingly of the Tamassee as "the closest thing to Eden we've got left" and considers it a "holy place" (53), but his truck bears an EARTH FIRST decal "printed beneath an upraised fist," a detail foreshadowing his willingness to resort to violence to preserve the river (39). About this person who taught Maggie photography, she observes that "Luke believed you saw the essentials in black and white, that color was nothing more than decoration and distraction," whereas Rash's fiction tends to avoid black-and-white perspectives in favor of subtle shadings of gray (95). As devoted as Luke is to the Tamassee, moreover, he is unable to commit to an enduring human relationship, and Maggie considers him deficient in empathy (94), a key term in Rash's work. Maggie herself is likewise impaired emotionally by her inability to forgive her father and by her tendency to distance herself from others, as symbolized by the camera that intervenes between her and the people or objects she photographs. She fears making herself vulnerable and thus avoids "words of reconciliation and forgiveness" with her father, "because we both realized once you open your mouth to speak such words you open your heart too. You open it wide" (148–49). Yet it is Maggie's photo of the grief-stricken Herb Kowalsky that generates public sympathy for his cause.

Like *One Foot in Eden,* a title that indicates dual locations, *Saints* begins with Ruth's desire to stand "in two states at the same time," the Tamassee forming a boundary between South Carolina and Georgia (3). That image of duality is reflected in the novel's division into two parts, each composed of five chapters and each preceded by an italicized section, the first recounting Ruth's death and the second detailing the accident that befalls Ben and Maggie. For Ruth, however, the "states" between which she moves are life and death, although Rash's prism imagery in the lengthy lyrical sentence that concludes the book's opening section suggests that the two states may be time and eternity, "that the prism's colors are voices, voices that swirl around her head like a crown," the crown awarded to the faithful in heaven

(5). But Ruth is also said to become "part of the river" (5), immersed in the natural world on which human life depends. The natural and supernatural are yoked together here, as so often in Rash's writing, nature and the divine being mutual sources of human identity as he conceives of it. Part 1 ends with another borderline scene when Maggie and Allen walk onto a bridge over the Tamassee and kiss for the first time, confirming their growing romantic involvement.

Rash's portrait of nature in *Saints* is as complex and varied as that in his poetry, for nature can both nourish and destroy—or seem utterly indifferent. Like Rash, Maggie is attuned to the natural world, its beauty and danger. Upon her return to Oconee County, she notices that "the stars were . . . so much brighter than in Columbia. They looked closer up here as well, as though each one had been picked up and polished, then set nearer to the earth" (69). Maggie recognizes the region's flora: beardtongue and ragwort, birdfoot violets, sarvis, and mountain laurel (155, 228). Under Luke's tutelage she had read William Bartram and Horace Kephart, Edward Abbey, Wendell Berry, and Peter Mathiessen, as well as such poets as Hopkins and Wordsworth, whose phrase "spots of time" (a crucial concept for Rash, as referenced in chapter 3 of this study) she finds inadequate to the encounter with the "holy" she has at times experienced in and through nature (165). Maggie conceives of nature and God as intertwined, recalling "a Church of God preacher" who had denounced Luke and his followers as "'false prophets' who worshiped nature, not God, as though one," she adds, "were not part of the other" (165). Maggie also remembers Luke's offering her a dipper filled with water from the Tamassee while declaiming, "As the poet said, 'Drink and be whole again beyond confusion,'" one of several allusions Rash makes to Frost's "Directive" in his work (162).

Yet Maggie is likewise aware of nature's otherness and its capacity to harm human beings. Passing through the "wan and splotchy" light of the river gorge one foggy morning, she feels as if she has wandered into "the haunted wood of a sinister fairy tale": "Mushrooms lined the trail, including some Death's Caps" (84). The healing waters that Luke, alluding to Frost's poem, offers to Maggie are the same waters that drown Ruth Kowalsky at Wolf Cliff Falls. The cliff that gives this falls its name is as daunting as the one featured in Rash's later novel *The Cove*. "Wolf Cliff," Maggie remarks, "is a place where nature has gone out of its way to make humans feel insignificant" (81). Similarly Wolf Cliff Falls "dominate[s]" the photo Maggie takes of Ruth's father, who customarily "walk[s] with the confidence of a man who expected to dominate any situation" (132, 47). It is Kowalsky's "powerlessness" the photo unintentionally emphasizes (132). Additionally, readers learn, the river that kills Ruth nearly claimed Luke's life some years earlier, an incident witnessed by Maggie, to whom Luke says afterward, "Part of me wanted to stay. That hydraulic was like the still center of the universe. . . . It was like entering eternity" (64).

In this passage Luke's outlook again returns to nature, to the river, as mediator of Wordsworthian transcendent moments. For Maggie the Tamassee is also the place where she was baptized at age twelve, Ruth's age at the time of her death, that sacramental water leading Maggie's pastor to declare, "You're a child of God now . . . and ever always you will be" (218). A comparable duality (or multiplicity) of meanings attaches to Rash's fire imagery. The boiling water that horribly burns Ben is transmuted to the "bonding fires" that signify the comfort of home and of family unity across centuries, "both heirloom and talisman, nurtured and protected because generations recognized it for what it was—living memory" (111).

According to Maggie, in words applicable to Rash's own literary project, it is song and story, as presented in the "communal gatherings" at Billy Watson's store, that constitute "the closest thing to a bonding fire in Tamassee" (111). Living memory is conveyed in those songs, as in Rash's fiction and poetry. Maggie's aunt Margaret, her father's sister, resembles Rash's great-aunt in the poem "Morning Service: August, 1959" from *Among the Believers,* the closing lines of that poem echoed in Maggie's memory of the "balm" her aunt's voice offered after the "frightening" features of Pentecostal worship: "Sometimes as she sang I'd look out the open window and see the gravestones and wonder if even the dead listened" (116–17). Like that poem's great-aunt, Aunt Margaret has been recorded by the Smithsonian (220). Later in the novel, after a member of the local rescue squad, Randy Moseley, drowns when the portable dam collapses, his body also caught in the hydraulic, Aunt Margaret sings again at a memorial service below Wolf Cliff Falls. Her solo is the traditional hymn "Shall We Gather at the River," its refrain giving the novel its title. With Preacher Tilson reading the account of Jesus' resurrection in Matthew 28: 2–6 and then asking the congregation to pray that Randy's and Ruth's bodies may rise from the river, Rash once more employs the motif of raising the dead that is so prominent in his writing. Those prayers go unanswered until Randy's fraternal twin, Ronny, tosses dynamite into the river above the falls, thus freeing the trapped bodies. Rash has said of this scene: "I would not be the writer I am today had I not been raised Southern Baptist. I'm immersed in it [that tradition]. . . . In *Saints at the River* you have an actual resurrection of a body from a stream, an answer to prayer. Water is a potent symbol of death and resurrection."[23]

The religious dimension of *Saints* is heightened by Rash's drawing the book's epigraph from the chapter titled "The Value of Saintliness" in William James's *The Varieties of Religious Experience* (1902). That epigraph reads, "It [common sense] need not blame the votary; but it may be able to praise him only conditionally, as one who acts faithfully according to his [l]ights."[24] James, the founder of the philosophical movement known as pragmatism, appealed to common sense and the consequences of a belief or practice in determining its value. The words immediately preceding those quoted by Rash read as follows: "The fruits of religion . . . are, like all human products, liable to corruption by excess. Common sense must judge them" (372). James makes it clear, as orthodox Christianity likewise does, that saints are not flawless people; rather they are, as Martin Luther taught too, simultaneously saint and sinner, justified yet sinful. But James's emphasis on balance rather than excess allows readers to assess some of the flaws in characters such as Luke and Herb Kowalsky and Maggie herself.

James's chapter on saintliness affords readers intriguing perspectives on other features of Rash's work and his outlook on moral and religious life. Rash seems to share, for instance, James's belief in the individual's potential for moral reform and spiritual rebirth. According to James, "we never can be sure in advance of any man that his salvation by the way of love is hopeless. We have no right to speak of human crocodiles and boa-constrictors [James's own terms for evildoers] as of fixedly incurable beings" (390). Furthermore James's view of asceticism parallels in significant ways Rash's sense of Appalachian stoicism and of the world as decidedly postlapsarian. For James asceticism reflects "the belief that there is an element of real wrongness in this world, which is neither to be ignored nor evaded, but which must be squarely met and overcome by an appeal to the soul's heroic resources, and neutralized and cleansed away by suffering" (396), an example of which readers might well see in the deaths of Amy and Billy Holcombe in Isaac's section of *One Foot in Eden*.

In *Saints* Rash depicts two town meetings to dramatize some of the major conflicts among the characters. Ronny's dynamite brings closure to the conflict involving the recovery of Ruth's body, but not until the novel's final chapter, which shifts to present-tense narration, do readers learn that Maggie had reconciled with her father before his death, although that reconciliation occurs offstage and is handled too briefly to be very convincing or moving. Rash's shift to present tense suggests, however, that Maggie is now free of the burden of her past hard-heartedness. Both *One Foot in Eden* and *Saints* are books in which a corpse symbolizes the burden of the past, whether remote or recent, in the present. Just as Holland's mother believes her son's spirit will never rest until his remains are buried, so Ruth's mother, a Roman Catholic, believes "a person is in purgatory until the body is given Last Rites" (172).

At the end of *Saints*, Maggie again stands on the bridge where she and Allen stood at the close of part 1. Now Maggie thinks of her imminent return to Columbia and of her possible future there with Allen. Looking toward "the boulder-domed dark below the falls," a poetic phrase evoking nature's power and mystery, she concludes the novel by referring to "the river's vast and generous unremembering," another striking phrase (237). Given Rash's intense interest in the past, whether historical, cultural, or personal, the term *unremembering* indicates a significant contrast between human beings and other natural phenomena. Yet Rash also refers to that unremembering as "generous," a word he applies in the book's penultimate chapter not only to Aunt Margaret but also to Maggie herself. In the book's closing phrase, then, Rash simultaneously highlights both nature's beneficence and its indifference.

While this novel, as Sylvia Bailey Shurbutt has pointed out, "is certainly about the environmental issues that critics and reviewers have discussed, it is likewise a novel about family relationships, perceived failures, and guilt."[25] In particular the book deals with father-child relationships in the cases of Maggie's father, Allen Hemphill, Herb Kowalsky, and even Randy Moseley, about whose relationship to his children Allen inquires of Maggie. Maggie's impulse to be generous occurs, ironically, not in her relationship with her own father but in her desire that Herb "know beyond any doubt he had been a good father to his daughter" (228). During the novel's composition, Rash has said, his son had been injured after being hit by a car, an event that was "the undercurrent" in *Saints*: "I didn't realize until I pretty much finished that book that a lot of what I was writing about was my own fears as a parent."[26] Such an emotional undercurrent, together with the author's emphasis on environmental issues, helps enable *Saints* to speak to universal concerns, however rooted the novel may be in a specific geographical region.

For all its strengths as a "compelling story," in the words of one reviewer, this second novel is a lesser artistic achievement than Rash's first. In part, as that reviewer notes, Rash dilutes the novel's suspense by his "too liberal use of . . . foreshadowing," especially when Maggie's dying father, who had not attended the first town hall meeting, appears at the second to warn of the danger faced by the divers who will attempt to recover Ruth's body.[27] Moreover, as Susan Lefler observes, unlike the narrators in *One Foot in Eden*, almost all of whom are personally connected to Holland Winchester's murder, Maggie's distance from Ruth's death "creates a fundamentally different emotional climate" than that in Rash's first novel.[28] Rash has conceded the superiority of his first novel to his second: "if I had to choose between those

books, I would choose *One Foot in Eden.* . . . . The language is more interesting in *One Foot*—which is something that's important to me as a poet."[29] Yet
Saints remains an important novel in Rash's canon for its initial treatment of
environmental issues that would receive more extended analysis in *Serena*.

   Saints is also noteworthy because it was Rash's first novel to be published
by a major New York firm, Henry Holt, which two years later published
his third novel, *The World Made Straight* (2006).[30] Unlike Rash's first two
novels, his third is set in North Carolina (as are *Serena* and *The Cove*), but
like the first two, his third has a title with explicitly religious associations.
According to one of the book's main characters, the title phrase epitomizes
the thrust of Handel's *Messiah*: "the words proclaimed an order, *the crook-
edness of the world made straight.*"[31] In addition, as with *One Foot in Eden,*
this novel's epigraph, drawn from Herman Melville's famous chapter "The
Whiteness of the Whale" in *Moby-Dick,* speaks of the ambiguous intermingling of good and evil in this one color, which is representative of both "the
Christian's deity," writes Melville in the passage Rash quotes, and "things the
most appalling to mankind." The characters in this novel are likewise deeply
flawed admixtures of good and evil and inhabit a world desperately in need
of redemption. Reviewers greeted the book with high praise: fellow novelist
Donald Harington contended that it "establishes Rash as a major writer,"
while Lorraine Lopez in *Southern Review* described the novel as "completely
engrossing, the writing resonant and affecting" and lauded its dialogue as
"terse and sure, powerful in its pared-back authenticity," although she also
found Rash's portraits of women "disappointing."[32]

   The World Made Straight reveals an author experimenting with narrative techniques he had not previously attempted. Unlike Rash's first two
novels with their first-person narrators, this novel uses third-person limited
narration shared between two main characters, seventeen-year-old Travis
Shelton, a high school dropout, and thirty-eight-year-old Leonard Shuler,
who becomes a mentor and surrogate father to Travis. Like *Saints,* this book
is divided into two parts (of fifteen chapters rather than ten, though with
a nearly equal number of pages appearing in each part), a structure that
reinforces the sense of "balance" Shuler finds in *The Messiah* but that also
reflects the duality of good and evil in human nature (159). That doubleness
of vision is mirrored in Rash's alternation between past and present because
most of the chapters are preceded by excerpts from the nineteenth-century
ledgers of Dr. Joshua Candler, Shuler's great-great-grandfather, who may
have been present at the Shelton Laurel massacre during the Civil War and
thus may have participated in the killing of Travis's ancestors. Although the
ledgers, now in Leonard's possession, are Rash's invention, seeming to derive

from those Faulkner attributes to Isaac McCaslin's grandfather in *Go Down, Moses,* Dr. Candler was, in fact, a historical figure—and Rash's own great-great-great-great-grandfather.[33] Travis and Leonard investigate the history of this massacre of suspected Union sympathizers in Madison County while they also deal with personal crises there in the late 1970s, the novel's present time, a decade when mountain people began to get more heavily involved in the drug culture depicted in the novel, involvement that has since grown to epidemic proportions in Appalachia, as several of Rash's short stories also attest.

Among Rash's first three novels, *The World Made Straight* is the one in which consciousness of history receives its most intense and dramatic treatment. The Shelton Laurel massacre had haunted Rash for more than a quarter century before this book was published. "In the 1970s and '80s," he has said, "I started writing some poems about Shelton Laurel and got more and more interested in it."[34] He has also commented on the "decades of research" that contributed to the book, including research on nineteenth-century medicine.[35] On the novel's acknowledgments page he specifically credits Phillip Shaw Paludan's "excellent book" *Victims* for its account of the massacre, which took place in January 1863 (291). Paludan states that he was drawn to this event because of his interest in what Robert Jay Lifton called "the atrocity-producing situation," especially as that concept relates to the Holocaust and to the My Lai massacre by American troops in Vietnam.[36] Rash follows Paludan in referring to what he labels "one of the most troubling aspects of human history: the atrocities committed among people who have lived together for generations, as in Nazi Germany, Rwanda, Cambodia, Bosnia. As in Madison County, N.C., among my own ancestors, during the Civil War."[37] Rash had relatives on both sides of this bloodshed. In the 1890s the Rash and Shelton families were joined by marriage, and his paternal great-great-great-grandfather served in the Union army's North Carolina Mounted Infantry—a unit in which he did not enlist until after the Shelton Laurel massacre—while Candler served in the Confederacy's Sixty-Fourth North Carolina Infantry Regiment under Col. Lawrence Allen and Lt. Col. James A. Keith.[38] Rash thus had a very personal investment in this novel's depiction of events at Shelton Laurel, especially the murder of thirteen-year-old David Shelton, the youngest of the massacre's thirteen victims, who had forgiven his assailants and had pled for mercy only to be brutally killed.[39]

Rash opens the book with the first of twelve excerpts from Candler's fictional ledgers, which detail the patients he has seen, their complaints, the doctor's diagnosis, the patient's treatment, and the fee received. The initial entry is dated August 5, 1850; the last, June 17, 1863, though that one is followed by an additional undated entry in which a fellow soldier reports the doctor's death. Rash carefully constructs these entries so that they reveal Candler's intimate connection to the Shelton family and other Madison County residents over thirteen years, that number also the number of the murdered. The first entry, for example, records a visit to David Shelton's mother when she is seven months pregnant, while the fifth recounts the doctor's saving eight-year-old David from scarlet fever. The fourth lists James Shelton among the patients treated, and the sixth entry describes the sutures needed by Abney Shelton in May 1861 when he is injured in a fistfight following a vote on secession lost by the secessionists. That same entry mentions Lawrence Allen as suffering from aphonia, having lost his voice advocating for secession. The second entry begins by referring to Nance Franklin, age thirty-four in 1852, who lived to see three of her four sons killed before her eyes for being Confederate sympathizers, an event Leonard later uses to remind Travis that atrocities occurred on both sides (199). It was Nance Franklin who reportedly told her sons, "If you've got to die, die like a damned dog with your teeth in a throat,"[40] words paraphrased by Rash in his poem "Madison County: 1864" in *Among the Believers.* Rash makes this second ledger entry more poignant by having the doctor's fee paid by a day's work "repairing my roof by two oldest sons" (39). Another of these entries refers to Joe Woods, the oldest victim of the massacre. Familiarity with the particulars of events at Shelton Laurel obviously deepens the reader's appreciation for Rash's artistry in creating the ledgers and the multiple ironies the entries incorporate. By interweaving excerpts from the ledgers throughout the novel, Rash also keeps the reader mindful of the past and its continuing impact on Leonard and Travis.

The final entry in part 1 indicates that Candler is on furlough in Marshall, the county seat, in early January 1863. This is the first entry to include a place name, for the doctor has become a member of the Sixty-Fourth Regiment and no longer has a stable residence. All of his patients are women, as if to underscore the absence from home of able-bodied males. Part 2 then opens without a ledger entry, perhaps to emphasize that Candler, his furlough ended, has become too busy with wounded and ill soldiers to write. The four dated entries that appear in part 2 (entries dated from January 11, 1863, through June 17 of that year) lack the careful patterning of those in part 1 and thus appear more hurriedly written. Ages of patients are no longer given, only names, wound or injury, and treatment. Two of these entries mention amputations due to gunshot wounds, while three of the four refer to deaths from fever or combat, along with the doctor's need for more chloroform and laudanum. The names of several of the patients link them to the women treated in Marshall on January 2, whether the soldiers are father, husband, son, or other relative.

Of the four entries in part 2, it is the second, dated January 17, 1863, to which Leonard returns repeatedly, haunted by its concluding word, *Others* (185). Now in possession of his ancestor's ledgers, Leonard assumes that *Others* alludes to the women who were tortured to obtain information about the whereabouts of their male relatives as well as to the prisoners themselves. Both Leonard and Rash assume that Candler was present at the massacre, that perhaps he was even compelled to serve on the firing squad. In any case he would have witnessed the atrocity. Significantly Rash omits a ledger entry before the following chapter, as if to suggest the trauma the doctor has experienced, which silences him temporarily, the massacre itself literally unspeakable, though Leonard does refer briefly to an entry for January 19, one that the reader never sees.

The next entry the reader encounters is dated more than two months later and contains yet another of the many images of resurrection in Rash's work. The doctor reports that the sleeping soldiers have been covered overnight by snow. "Waked by a vexing dream at first light," the doctor notes, he hears the bugle sound reveille and watches "the land tremble alive as men rose in the whiteness as though arrayed in the fine linen of the righteous on the world's last day" (209). Ironically, by the final dated entry in June, one of those "resurrected" soldiers has been killed. In that last of his entries, Candler writes that he, too, has been shot, adding the following comments: "Much pain as God is just. Refuse anodynes. Want mind clear to pray for my soul, ask forgiveness for what cannot be hidden from my Maker" (223). With these words Rash underscores the doctor's sense of culpability, whatever his specific role at Shelton Laurel.

Candler's desire for reconciliation and forgiveness finds a counterpart in the relationship that develops between Leonard Shuler and Travis Shelton more than one hundred years later. Leonard is a former history teacher who lost his job when a student he had failed for cheating planted drugs in Leonard's car. Travis is a high school dropout whom Leonard recognizes as possessing a bright mind, evidenced by the boy's intellectual curiosity and his capacity for reflection. As Leonard's surname indicates (the German for school is *Schule,* while *Schüler* means pupil or scholar), he is both teacher and student, learning even as he mentors Travis. Alienated by the loss of his job and the dissolution of his marriage, which also leads to his separation from his young daughter, Leonard supports himself by selling alcohol and drugs, having been set up in that business by Carlton Toomey. Travis first meets Leonard after stealing marijuana plants he discovers on Toomey's land while trout fishing, later selling the plants to Leonard. Like Maggie Glenn of *Saints,* Travis is estranged from his father, a tobacco farmer, so as the book unfolds, Leonard gradually becomes a father figure to Travis.

The novel's opening chapter, a revision of Rash's O. Henry Award-winning story "Speckled Trout," introduces not only Travis, Leonard, and Carlton Toomey but also such secondary characters as Travis's friend Shank, Carlton's son Hubert, and Dena, a thirty-four-year-old drug addict who has been living with Leonard in his trailer for some thirteen months but who has had a previous involvement with the Toomeys, whose surname suggests their—and their drugs'—death-dealing propensity. In fact the taut suspense Rash creates in this initial chapter leaves readers expecting that Travis may be murdered by Carlton. Instead Toomey cuts his Achilles tendon, telling him, "we got to be certain sure you don't forget there's a price to be paid for stealing" (43). Travis thus joins Billy Holcombe and Sheriff Alexander among Rash's limping protagonists.

The novel's present-day action covers less than a year, from early August 1978 to early April 1979. By late August, after an angry confrontation with his father, Travis has moved into Leonard's trailer, which enables Rash to delineate the growing relationship between Shelton and Shuler. By this point Travis has also developed a romantic interest in Lori Triplett, a former high school classmate. Lori's family is among the most impoverished in the county, and Lori views education as her way to escape that poverty. She plans not only to earn her high school diploma but also to pursue a degree as a certified nursing assistant at Asheville-Buncombe Technical College. Although Travis often chafes at Lori's insistence that he, too, pursue higher education once he attains the GED degree that Leonard encourages him to complete, Rash uses all three of these characters to demonstrate the intelligence of mountain people and the importance of education to them. Leonard had graduated some twenty years earlier from the same high school Travis and Lori now attend and then had gone on to earn a degree at the University of North Carolina at Chapel Hill. Even Carlton Toomey is portrayed as bright and quick-witted, though he has learned to seem the ignorant hillbilly, like the Clemson-educated Billy Watson of *Saints,* who "play[s] Snuffy Smith to fleece tourists" (21). The value of education is a recurring motif in Rash's fiction, and *The World Made Straight* is in many ways a bildungsroman.

Leonard's mentoring of Travis begins even before the teenager moves into Leonard's trailer, for in the opening chapter Shuler uses the Confederate flag T-shirt Travis wears to illustrate his ignorance: "If you'd worn it up here in the 1860s it could have gotten you killed, and by your own blood kin," he explains (28).[41] Travis had also mistakenly assumed that Yankees had done the killing at Shelton Laurel. One of the misconceptions about southern history that Rash seeks to correct here, especially about the history of the mountain South, is the assumption of monolithic support for the Confederacy. Once Travis's curiosity is aroused, he begins reading about the Civil War and asking for material about Shelton Laurel, which he and Leonard visit in chapter 5, taking Leonard's metal detector. There Travis locates a small pair of wire-rim glasses, one frame still holding its lens, "a coin of glass" (90). Because of the size of the glasses, Travis immediately assumes they belonged to David Shelton, an hypothesis later confirmed by Leonard's reading in Candler's ledgers (117). For Travis the glasses become a talisman, providing a connection across time. As an instrument of vision, they symbolize his capacity for empathy, a word highlighted in his first encounter with Leonard (23). On a second visit to Shelton Laurel in chapter 11 on the massacre's anniversary, he puts on the glasses, feeling "closer to it [the massacre] somehow" by seeing it, however partially, from David Shelton's perspective (205). Rash's work is meant to promote the kind of empathy that Travis experiences here, the ability to feel the suffering of others and to act to prevent or alleviate that suffering.

After chapter 11 the novel's pace accelerates, the last four chapters focusing on a three-day period in April when the smoldering conflicts between Rash's protagonists and the Toomeys erupt. Dena is one major source of those conflicts. Her drug addiction binds her to the Toomeys because they supply her with money or pills in exchange for sexual acts in which Dena is physically abused or debased. In chapter 9 Carlton appears at Leonard's trailer to take Dena away for a weekend of such activity. At the end of chapter 11, when Leonard and Travis return from Shelton Laurel, Dena has packed up her belongings and moved in with the Toomeys, in part because Leonard has stopped selling drugs. That decision is one of several significant improvements in Leonard's life resulting from his relationship with Travis, a decision that gravely displeases Carlton, who will thus lose profits from Shuler's sales.

But Leonard had begun to change almost from the moment Travis moved into the trailer. According to Leonard, who had been living a kind of death-in-life existence, "Travis had brought time into the trailer with him" (71), the boy's presence gradually prompting him to reengage with history, both literally and figuratively, and to assume responsibility for his life. Leonard's ex-wife, Kera, had accused him of "living in the passive voice, letting others make choices so if things went wrong he didn't have to bear the blame" (54). Kera had also wondered if Leonard's passivity was motivated not so much by fear of blame as by selfishness: "you want to be left alone and never have to worry about anyone but yourself" (156). In his relationship with Travis, however, Leonard transcends such egocentricity, in part because he wants to make amends for his ancestor's role at Shelton Laurel. At times, then, the mentor-pupil dynamic between the two undergoes a reversal, with Travis insuring Leonard's growth just as Leonard does Travis's.

The novel's four climactic chapters begin calmly enough with Travis's passing the GED exam, but the ensuing celebration quickly deteriorates when he confronts his father, who refuses to attend the dinner party arranged by Lori. During that confrontation Travis's father reveals that Shuler is a descendant of those who massacred the Sheltons, information that Leonard has withheld. Angry at his father and Lori and Leonard, Travis seeks out Shank, who drives Travis and another friend to the Toomeys' farmhouse (a destination of which Travis is unaware) to purchase quaaludes. There Travis discovers Dena tied to a bedpost and threatens to "put the law" on Carlton unless she is released. Carlton insists, however, that Dena owes him $1,400 for the pills she has consumed since January. When the other boys leave, Travis stays behind, hidden in the shadows, and later uproots the Toomeys' newly planted marijuana crop, rescues Dena, and takes the Toomeys' car to escape. These actions precipitate the violence that culminates in the deaths of the Toomeys and Leonard after Leonard forces the truck in which he is riding with the Toomeys off the highway and down a steep embankment. But that fatal accident occurs only after Leonard has enabled Travis and Dena to escape.

The book's final chapter describes Dena's departure by bus from Marshall, Travis's discovery of the accident scene (where he finds the dead Carlton still clutching the money Leonard offered the Toomeys, money he takes and sends to Dena), and Travis's subsequent drive toward Lori's home, a destination that implies his future reconciliation with her. Travis's gift of the money contrasts sharply with his acquisitive stance in the novel's opening chapter, in which he steals marijuana plants and fishes for speckled trout because of the cash they will bring. Even though Travis realizes that Dena may just spend the money he sends on pills, he thinks of his action as "one thing done right, maybe even a kind of beginning" (288). The book's closing sentence, with its echo of the novel's title and its imagery of ascent, confirms such hopefulness: "The road curved briefly, then straightened as he began the long ascent north to Antioch" (289).

The World Made Straight recapitulates and extends thematic concerns evident throughout Rash's fiction, among them his focus on war and its consequences, his view of human nature as deeply flawed yet capable of redemption, his emphasis on historical consciousness, his sense of religious mystery at work in nature, and his growing interest in what Shuler calls "landscape as destiny," which becomes a prominent subject in *The Cove* as well (156). Rash invokes historical consciousness of war not only through the book's treatment of the Shelton Laurel massacre but also through allusions to World War II and, indirectly, the Trojan War. At one point Leonard reads to Travis a quotation by Simone Weil: "Force is as pitiless to the man who possesses it, or thinks he does, as it is to its victims: the second it crushes, the first it intoxicates. Those who use it and those who endure it are turned to stone. . . . a soul which has entered the province of force will not escape this except by a miracle" (162). Although Rash does not identify the source of this passage, it appears in Weil's essay "The *Iliad* or the Poem of Force," first published in early 1941 after the Nazi occupation of France.[42] Later in the novel Leonard recalls Weil's remarking that "the true object of war is the warrior's soul," another statement from the same essay (206). Weil's theological concerns, indicated by such words as *miracle* and *soul*, become increasingly apparent as her essay unfolds. Like Edwin Muir in the poem that gave Rash's first novel its title, Weil sees the fallen world as a source of virtues otherwise unavailable to humanity. Near the end of her essay, Weil writes, in a passage not quoted by Rash, "the sense of human misery is a pre-condition of justice and love."[43] Rash's use of Weil thus reinforces the novel's religious dimension and reminds readers of the recurrence of war across human history, a repetition of violence consistent with Travis's—and presumably Rash's—concept of time: "the notion that time didn't so much pass as *layer over things,* as if under the world's surface the past was still occurring" (86). The question Rash implicitly raises is how humanity can avoid perpetuating the violence so pervasive in the history of our species—and seemingly in its very nature. His own historical research on atrocities, the author notes, led him not to "understanding" but only to "awareness": "That may be the best that any work of historical fiction has to offer . . . a chance to grapple with the mysteries and complexities of the past, in hopes of seeing the present a little clearer."[44]

That sense of mysteries and complexities is certainly evident in Rash's portrait of Carlton Toomey, whom one reviewer calls "one of the most appalling villains in contemporary fiction."[45] Yet brutal as Toomey ultimately proves to be, Rash depicts him as a complex mixture of good and evil. He is capable of adopting another's viewpoint, of empathizing with Leonard and Travis, and of singing a gospel song as "only a child of God could" (50). In fact he claims his singing has converted enough sinners and strengthened enough "backsliders" that God "will cut me some slack in other areas" (179). "I guess I'm somewheres betwixt and between, like any another man," he tells Leonard (50). But he also insists on his right to do exactly as he pleases with Dena because of the money she owes him. In that regard he thinks only in terms of abstract "justice," ignoring the claims of mercy and the acts of simple kindness Rash portrays in Leonard's relationship with Dena. Toomey dies with Leonard's savings clutched in his hand while humming the hymn "Will There Be Any Stars in My Crown" (281).

However ironic the juxtaposition of these traits and images may be, that hymn directs readers to the mystery of God's love for sinners, to the wonder of God's redemptive grace. The professor whom Leonard recalls playing Handel's *Messiah* in a music appreciation class was a World War II veteran who had lost a leg and half his right hand on D-Day. The "magnificent order" Leonard finds in Handel's oratorio had led Professor Heddon to stand before his students "holding his right hand up, what remained of his palm open as though to absolve them. There is beauty in this world, he told them," Leonard remembers, "more beauty than any of us can fathom, and we must not ever forget this" (159, 160). Leonard's Pentecostal mother had told him something similar as she gazed at the mountains, finding in nature a revelation of that beauty and order: "She'd told him that sometimes a Bible or church wasn't enough" (104). The practice of speaking in tongues among Pentecostal congregations attests to the ineffable, to experiences that transcend human powers of expression. As Rash writes in the poem "Sunday Evening at Middlefork Creek Pentecostal Church," "Like poets, they [the parishioners] know a fallen world's / words fail a pure vision" (*Among the Believers* 22).

This embrace of mystery, of the ineffable, is central to Rash's artistic vision and his religious consciousness. It may be this stance that leads him to have characters in both this novel and *Saints at the River* quote Friedrich Nietzsche's contention that "what can be spoken is already dead in the heart" (143; *Saints* 217). While hyperbolic, this claim may also contribute to Rash's portrait of Leonard's sense of wonder in the closing pages of *The World Made Straight,* an emotion he links to Professor Heddon's comments on *The Messiah* and one Leonard envisions sharing with his daughter through "a pearl of rain held in his open palm," an image that parallels the open palm that the music professor raises (282–83; cf. 275).

Running counter, however, to Leonard's sense of wonder at life's beauty and possibilities is his sense of "landscape as destiny," a topic about which Rash has spoken to several interviewers. On one occasion he remarked, "I think the landscape a person is born into has a huge effect on his or her perception of reality."[46] On another he said, "I really believe . . . landscape must affect the way people see the world. There's a certain fatalism I've seen in my own family that I think comes in large part from being in the mountains, from a landscape that lacks that long vision, from the mountains always rising up and reminding you how small you are," though he goes on to acknowledge that the mountain landscape can also be seen as "womblike and nurturing."[47] In Leonard's case the mountains create the former impression, with their "brooding presence," their "light-starved ridges and coves" (72). For Leonard the phrase *landscape as destiny* means "the sense of being closed in, of human limitation," which he views as "so different from the Midwest, where the possible sprawled bright and endless in every direction" (156–57). Leonard recognizes the paradoxical "comfort" that assuming one's impotence can bring, but he resists the rejection of personal responsibility that such an outlook entails. Moreover his sojourn in the Midwest, where he lost his teaching job, has convinced him "how truly oppressive the openness [of the landscape] was" (108). Whereas Leonard's mother, from whom the mountains elicit "devotion," does not share his sense of being hemmed in (159), Maggie Glenn of *Saints* does, feeling "claustrophobic" amid the mountains after Ben's accident, "as though the mountains had moved closer together since we'd been at the hospital, and would keep on moving closer until they finally suffocated me" (130). As the following chapter will show, this notion of landscape as destiny is one to which Rash returns at greater length in *The Cove*. It is a notion seemingly at odds with the author's tendency to emphasize the moral choices his characters make and the responsibility they bear for those choices, a major theme in all three of the novels examined in this chapter.

CHAPTER 5

Serena and *The Cove*

Rash's literary reputation reached new heights with the publication of *Serena* (2008), a finalist for the PEN/Faulkner Award and widely recognized as his finest novel to date. Reviewing the book for the *New York Times,* Janet Maslin wrote of its "many wonders" and its "haunting power," while suggesting that it would "prompt instant interest" in Rash's earlier novels.[1] Jay Parini in his review for the *Guardian* referred to *Serena* as a "brilliant novel" and "spectacular book" and praised its "beautifully wrought" plot, though he found Serena herself "more like a creature of legend than a real person—a symbol, not a human being."[2] The book won popular success as well. It appeared on the *Publishers Weekly* "Best Books of the Year" list, ranked seventh among Amazon.com's one hundred best books of 2008, and was on the "best of 2008" lists of the *Washington Post* and the *San Francisco Chronicle*.

Like Rash's fifth novel, *The Cove* (2012), *Serena* is a historical novel set in western North Carolina, but whereas *The Cove* focuses on a period of roughly three months as World War I nears its end, *Serena* covers approximately three years from 1929 to 1932 and offers a vividly detailed portrait of the timber industry and its devastating impact on the landscape and ecology of Haywood and Jackson Counties west of Asheville. The book also depicts that industry's struggle against those individuals and groups working to establish the Great Smoky Mountains National Park. Among Rash's diverse cast of characters are several historical figures, including Horace Kephart, author of *Our Southern Highlanders* (1913) and an ardent advocate for the park; Horace Albright, U.S. secretary of the interior; Charles A. Webb, publisher and editor of the Asheville newspaper; and Cornelia Vanderbilt and her British husband, John Cecil, at whose Biltmore estate one of the book's chapters is set. At the center of this novel, however, are the fictional George and Serena Pemberton, who operate the Boston Lumber Company with all the ruthlessness of nineteenth-century robber barons; Rachel Harmon, who bears Pemberton's illegitimate child; and several other superbly delineated characters, most notably Sheriff McDowell and Serena's henchman Galloway. Ambitious in scope and design, thematically complex, rich in dramatic incident and suspense, *Serena* is Rash's masterpiece. As the author himself has observed, "*Serena* for me is the best novel I will ever write. . . . That's the book I am proudest of."[3] Rash worked on the novel for three years, completing at least twelve full drafts of the book.[4] From one of those drafts, as chapter 2 of this study noted, he drew the material that became the novella "Pemberton's Bride," published in *Chemistry and Other Stories.*

One measure of the novel's ambition is its wide range of allusions and what Rash has described as his intent to give *Serena* "the feel of an Elizabethan drama."[5] That intention is implicit in the book's epigraph, "A hand, that with a grasp may grip the worlde," a line drawn from Christopher Marlowe's lesser-known play *The Massacre at Paris,* in which the words are spoken by the Duke of Guise, who fomented the persecution of French Protestants that led to the St. Bartholomew's Day massacre of 1572. In the two lines immediately preceding Rash's epigraph, the Duke declares, "Give me a look, that when I bend the brows, / Pale death may walk in furrows of my face," a remark consistent with the murderous impulses and actions of Serena and Pemberton.[6] Marlowe's play, like Rash's novel, is littered with corpses, that carnage and Serena's cruelty leading critic Joyce Compton Brown to link the book to Jacobean revenge tragedy, especially Thomas Kyd's *The Spanish Tragedy.*[7] But, as Brown also points out, Rash's choice of epigraph is likely meant to evoke "Marlowe's Faustian concept," what Harry Levin called "the overreacher" in his study of Marlowe's plays.[8] Serena becomes the epitome of such overreaching, and it is to her that the novel's epigraph best applies. Shakespeare's influence is likewise apparent in Rash's conception of the book. Numerous reviewers and critics have commented on Serena's resemblance to Lady Macbeth, and Brown reports that Rash intended some of the loggers' remarks to suggest those of "Shakespeare's wise fools," a parallel evident in one of the men's motley clothing and his later acquisition of cap and bells from a visiting carnival juggler.[9]

These Renaissance influences and allusions are complemented by classical and modern ones, especially Rash's use of the loggers to form a chorus reminiscent of Greek tragedy, a chorus that comments on the Pembertons' actions and thus offers a set of contrasting values. That chorus also enables Rash to incorporate the vernacular speech of the region he knows so well and provides opportunities to modulate the novel's tone by including elements of humor that counterbalance the grim realities of the Pembertons' conduct. For all the brutality of character and event in this novel's portrait of the Pembertons and Galloway, Serena contains more humor than any of the author's other novels. Among the book's additional classical allusions are quotations from Euripides's *Medea* and Cicero's *De Oratore,* as well as a reference to the shield of Achilles, depicted in book 18 of Homer's *Iliad,* while Rash's allusions to American writers invoke some of the major texts of the nation's literature: Melville's *Moby-Dick,* Mark Twain's *Adventures of Huckleberry Finn,* F. Scott Fitzgerald's *The Great Gatsby,* and Faulkner's *Go Down, Moses.*

Of equal or perhaps greater significance thematically is Rash's evocation of biblical perspectives and values, whether through the names he assigns characters, such as Rachel and her son, Jacob, or through Reverend Bolick's denunciation of Pemberton in chapter 17, or through the loggers' seriocomic dialogue on loving one's neighbor in chapter 25. Moreover the novel's italicized coda, set in October 1975, records an act of retribution consistent with the biblical motif of divine judgment and punishment of evildoers. Whatever the nature of Rash's allusions and influences, however, they all help to make *Serena* a book both distinctively of its region and decidedly universal in characters and actions and themes.

In speaking of this novel's originating image, Rash has said that it "came in a vision, a tall woman on horseback, silhouetted against the sky." "I realized," he adds, "I was seeing her through the eyes of another character, who looked at her with fear. And I realized it was her husband."[10] Yet in the book's opening chapter, he gives readers ample reason to fear both of the Pembertons. That chapter begins with a two-sentence paragraph exhibiting Rash's economy of means and his ability to immerse readers quickly in suspenseful situations: "When Pemberton returned to the North Carolina mountains after three months in Boston settling his father's estate, among those waiting on the train platform was a young woman pregnant with Pemberton's child. She was accompanied by her father, who carried beneath his shabby frock coat a bowie knife sharpened with great attentiveness earlier that morning so it would plunge as deep as possible into Pemberton's heart."[11] That bowie knife is one of several knives that figure prominently in the novel's violence, including the hunting knife that Serena has given her husband as a wedding present, a weapon with which he coldly eviscerates Rachel's father, who has been drinking heavily and who is, Pemberton recognizes, inexperienced in fighting with a knife. This initial scene, reminiscent of the shooting of the drunken Boggs by Colonel Sherburn in chapter 21 of *Huckleberry Finn,* also demonstrates Serena's callousness, for she tells Abe Harmon that he and his daughter are fortunate to have had the girl "breed" with Pemberton—who does not even recall Rachel's name—and then urges her husband to settle this dispute with his knife. Following Harmon's death Serena returns the bowie knife to Rachel, urging her to sell it to help support her unborn child. "It's all you'll ever get from my husband and me" (10), she insists, an assertion later proven false despite the complete confidence with which Serena utters it. The bowie knife, moreover, ultimately becomes the instrument of Serena's own death.

The image of the heart with which Rash concludes his opening paragraph invites readers to consider the heartlessness of the Pembertons' words and actions, both in this chapter and throughout the novel, Serena consistently surpassing her husband in this regard. The heart's conventional association with love likewise enables Rash to contrast Serena and Rachel as the two characters' personalities steadily unfold. Ten of the book's thirty-seven chapters focus on Rachel, including three of the first nine and four of the last eleven. She is thus clearly meant as a foil to Serena, particularly after Serena's miscarriage while pregnant with a son leaves her unable to bear other children. Although she initially tells herself not to love Jacob ("Don't love anything that can be taken away" [51]), part 1 closes with the seriously ill Rachel, who has carried her even sicker son to the doctor late one night, conceding that the doctor is right when he says, "You must love that child dear as life." "I tried not to," Rachel acknowledges. "I just couldn't find a way to stop myself" (97). Given Flannery O'Connor's influence on Rash's work, his portrait of Rachel at this point may owe something to O'Connor's question about the protagonist of her first novel, *Wise Blood*: "Does one's integrity ever lie in what he is not able to do?"—a question to which O'Connor responds, "I think that usually it does."[12]

In contrast to Rachel, the Pembertons, in their self-absorption and greed, seem characters out of an Ayn Rand novel. At the same time, they embody some of the worst features of the years preceding the Great Recession that began in the United States in 2008, an economic disaster from which the nation is still slowly recovering in 2013, one fueled by the laissez-faire business policies of the George W. Bush presidency. That same presidential administration proposed selling timbering rights in national parks and forests, and thus Rash's novel, in dealing with the struggle to establish the Great Smoky Mountains National Park, likewise addresses current environmental concerns, not only those involving deforestation but also those resulting from the devastating practice of mountaintop-removal coal mining. Even though western North Carolina is not itself a coal-mining region, it is impossible to read Rash's descriptions of the environmental destruction caused by clear-cutting the forests without envisioning the consequences of mountaintop removal in Appalachia. Rash employs the term *wasteland* at least seven times in portraying that devastation and uses the phrase "stumps and slash" even more often to describe what remains on the landscape, the term *slash* linking that despoiling of the natural environment to the Pembertons' and Galloway's murders of people. In addition the pattern of absentee land ownership that the Boston Lumber Company represents has long plagued Appalachia, with such corporations extracting the region's rich natural resources while impoverishing its residents. When publisher Webb asks the timber industry's representatives "Can't you give something back to the people of this region?" his appeal has no effect on the Pembertons (137). In fact, as Serena observes one of their business partners, Buchanan, indicating a willingness to sell land for the national park, she decides that Buchanan must be killed and enlists her husband to shoot Buchanan on a hunting trip—though she is more than willing to commit the murder herself. "Another time for me, then," she calmly states as the chapter in which this plot is hatched concludes (141). Whereas the death of Abe Harmon, though needless, can be seen as an act of self-defense, no such extenuating circumstance applies in this case. Buchanan's death precipitates a series of murders that culminate with Pemberton's own death in the book's final chapter, a murder necessitated, according to Serena, by Pemberton's betrayal when he sends Rachel money to help her and Jacob escape from Serena and Galloway.

The Pembertons' predatory attitude toward nature as well as other people contrasts sharply with the attitude of Rachel and of Rash himself. For the Pembertons, as for many of those whom Rash criticizes through his portraits of Serena and George, nature has value almost solely in monetary terms. Significantly the first action Serena undertakes in the logging camp involves her accurately estimating, in a wager with a worker named Bilded, the number of board feet in a large tree previously left standing because it shaded the camp's office. To determine the winner of this bet, the tree must be cut down. In itself the tree has no value for Serena, nor does she consider its utility in providing shade for those employed in the office. Like his wife, Pemberton views natural phenomena not in terms of their beauty or their right to exist apart from their usefulness to human beings but rather in mercenary terms. Encountering dogwood, mountain laurel, and rhododendron, for instance, all known for their attractive springtime blossoms, he thinks only "someday soon there'd be a poison to eradicate such valueless trees and shrubs" (231).

Pemberton's desire to shoot a mountain lion, one of the plot elements helping to unify the book, reinforces his indifference to nature's well-being, for readers learn early on that these creatures (referred to as panthers or "painters" by the mountaineers) are virtually extinct, the last one found in

North Carolina having been killed in 1920 (6). Pemberton offers a twenty-dollar gold coin to anyone who can locate a lion for him, an offer that recalls Ahab's in *Moby-Dick,* Pemberton's coin even being called at one point a "gold doubloon" (105). But whereas Ahab seeks the white whale because it has reaped away his leg and because it becomes for him an embodiment of all evil, Pemberton's motive is impulsive and whimsical, his proposed action further threatening that species' very survival in an entire state. While Ahab's motives, however misguided, have a heroic dimension, Pemberton's are self-centered and trivial. It is the prospect of shooting this prey, moreover, that ultimately enables Serena and Galloway to lure him to his death.

As the book's imagery and action emphasize, the Pembertons dispense death to nature as well as to other people. The stumps already present when Serena arrives in North Carolina, Rash writes, "resembled grave markers in a recently vacated battlefield" (23). Such death imagery recurs when snow-covered "slash piles" are compared to "burial mounds" and when, near novel's end, the denuded landscape appears to be "the skinned hide of some huge animal" (63, 333). When Serena trains a Mongolian Birkute eagle to hunt rattlesnakes—creatures that she sees as bad only because they slow the crew's work and thus reduce profits, not because the snakes harm the loggers—she disrupts the ecological balance that had kept the workers' housing largely rat-free. Similarly the silting of streams caused by clear-cutting leads to the water's inability to sustain trout, which are then unavailable for consumption at Pemberton's thirtieth birthday party in the book's penultimate chapter. The Pembertons' disregard for nature's vitality is thus shown to be self-destructive, a danger to human well-being.

Unlike George and Serena, Rachel attends to nature's beauty and practices principles of land use that promote sustainability instead of the pattern of exploitation and flight that characterizes the Pembertons and their counterparts in the timber industry, with their Nietzschean will to power and their bottom-line mentality. The Harmons, like Rash's ancestors, have lived on their land since the mid-1700s, maintaining its health, not transforming it into a wasteland. Readers see Rachel gathering ginseng, for example, but carefully covering up the plants' berries so they will reproduce another year. Rachel notices Queen Anne's lace shining with "beaded blossoms of dew" and thinks how in spring "dogwood branches swayed and sparkled as if harboring clouds of white butterflies" (40, 42). One of her fondest memories of her father revolves around his showing her a luna moth, an emblem of nature's beauty. When Serena and Galloway force Rachel to flee her home, she first places Jacob's hand on the ground outside their cabin: "'Don't ever forget what it feels like, Jacob,' she whispered, and let her hand touch the

ground as well," thereby affirming her connection not only to the land but
to the past (272). Unlike those Rash characters who feel shut in by mountains, including Rachel's mother, who left the family when her daughter was
five, Rachel finds the landscape "sheltering, . . . as if the mountains were
huge hands, hard but gentle hands that cupped around you, protecting and
comforting, the way she imagined God's hands would be" (197–98). She
responds similarly to the mountains near Seattle, to which she escapes with
Jacob, finding that "their stillness settled inside her like a healing balm"
(330). In all these ways Rachel is attuned to nature as a living, sustaining
presence, worthy of preservation in its turn. Rash's novel should be read,
then, at least in part, through the lens provided by ecocritical approaches to
literature. In his fiction and poetry alike, he captures the beauty and fragility
of the natural world, as when in *Serena* he describes a flight of goldfinches:
"the flock expanded like gold cloth unraveling, . . . their passage through the
charred valley as ephemeral as a candle flame waved over an abyss" (334).

Just as the Pembertons disregard or discount the future, especially of the
landscapes they decimate, so they ignore the past, a stance that clearly sets
them at odds with Rash's worldview, with its frequent forays into historical
fiction and its consciousness of the past's ongoing presence. Serena is particularly adamant about the past's irrelevance, acting and speaking in accordance
with that conviction, although she unconsciously demonstrates the opposite
perspective insofar as she strives to erase the fruits of Pemberton's earlier relationship with Rachel. Her parents and siblings having died in the influenza
epidemic of 1918 when she was just sixteen, Serena had the family home
and all its contents, including photographs, burned before she moved east.
When Wilkie, one of the Pembertons' business partners, asks to hear more
about her father, who had owned the Vulcan Lumber Company in Colorado,
Serena replies with astounding indifference, "Why? . . . He's dead now and
of no use to any of us," a remark with which Rash concludes chapter 2 (38).
And after Serena has mastered the eagle she trains, she sees in that raptor
"what we want," she tells Pemberton: "To be like this. No past or future,
pure enough to live totally in the present" (87). That such an outlook would
annul distinctively human consciousness and is neither desirable nor possible becomes evident when Serena unveils her long-standing intention, once
the Pembertons have finished logging their holdings in North Carolina, to
move to Brazil, where virgin mahogany forests await cutting. What makes
that country particularly attractive to Serena is "its laissez-faire attitude toward businesses" and the fact that it has "no law but nature's law," presumably that of survival of the fittest, an assumption in keeping with the social
Darwinism that pervades Serena's thought and action (215, 29). For a time

Pemberton imitates Serena in detaching himself from the past, as when he burns, without opening them, letters sent from Boston by his family. But his awareness of Jacob, the child he will never have with Serena, finally draws him out of the closed circle he and Serena form into a relationship encompassing both past and future—though it does so at the cost of his life.

At times Rash strains credibility in his portrait of Serena, whose utter indifference to the potential consequences of her murderous actions may seem improbable, though Serena would not be the first person to believe that her wealth and social position insulate her from any accountability or to forget that actions sometimes have unforeseen consequences. In any case the casual manner in which she orders the killings of Buchanan, Campbell, and Harris, among others, and her own cutting of Widow Jenkins's throat leave no doubt about her cruelty. Even Pemberton, who carries out the murder of Buchanan, comes to "believe her capable of anything," a conclusion he reaches after she proposes Harris's death (244). In her sheer amorality, Serena becomes a figure of mythic proportions, perceived as godlike by Wilkie, who provokes Reverend Bolick's ire by claiming of her, "She'll never be crucified by the rabble" (134). Dr. Cheney and the loggers, on the other hand, consider Serena evil incarnate, Cheney remarking that she "milked the fangs [of the dead rattlesnakes] and coated her tongue with the poison," while the loggers speak of fire, with its association with Hell, as both of the Pembertons' "natural element" (102, 322). Rash confirms this impression at the time of Serena's death when a "superstitious" guard at her home in Brazil testifies that "a garland of white fire flamed around her head" (371). Earlier in the novel, the narrator describes Serena on her white horse as "appear[ing] to ride the air itself" (68), an image he later applies to Serena and Pemberton, as well as to Galloway (who wears rattlesnake rattles on his hat), in the closing sentence of chapter 23: "Then they were gone as if consumed by the air itself" (229). "Spirits of air" is a term often used to refer to witches and other demonic beings, a concept Rash seems to invoke here to underscore these characters' preternatural evil. In so doing he sometimes shifts the novel away from historical realism—and even the sensationalism of the southern gothic tradition—toward a moral allegory akin to Hawthorne's.

Yet Rash also attributes much of the wanton destructiveness of the Pembertons' conduct to their privileged social position and their total indifference to the well-being of the loggers, whom the Depression makes readily expendable and replaceable. The animosity between Pemberton and Sheriff McDowell, for example, first mentioned in the opening chapter but unexplained there, is later traced to Pemberton's reckless driving in Waynesville, for which he is arrested and briefly jailed. Rachel comments similarly on Serena and her horse: "She and that gelding would go right over whoever got in their way and not give the least notice they'd trampled someone into the dirt" (132). Like Daisy and Tom in *The Great Gatsby*—the Daisy who runs over and kills Myrtle in Gatsby's car—the Pembertons are what Nick Carraway calls "careless people": "they smashed up things and creatures and then retreated back into their money or their vast carelessness, or whatever it was that kept them together."[13] For the Pembertons that bond is what one critic calls their "unbridled hubris and limitless ambition."[14] As do many of Rash's other works, *Serena* draws attention to social class differences and economic inequalities. The ornate saddle on Serena's Arabian, for instance, "cost[s] more than a logger earned in a year" (21). More important, however, the Pembertons' wealth, as later chapters show, enables Serena and her husband to evade justice by corrupting the presumed guardians of the law. The main reason that the decent-hearted company accountant, Campbell, must be hunted down and killed after he abruptly leaves his job is that he "knows who we've paid off and what for," admits Serena (226). In such situations the autocratic control that the Pembertons exercise is less an expression of metaphysical evil than a reflection of historical conditions in Appalachia— and elsewhere in America—in the early twentieth century, when coal camps were often subjected to brutal domination by Baldwin-Felts detectives and other private security personnel and when efforts to unionize coal miners and textile workers were frequently met with intimidation, firings, and overt violence. Rash's first book of poems, *Eureka Mill,* details some of these matters as they affected textile workers.

Significantly, although Rash titles *Serena* for its female villain, it is the loggers themselves whose perspective he privileges by his pervasive use of them as this novel's chorus. Rash's intricate knowledge of the tools and equipment of the logging industry, as well as of the fatal occupational hazards the men confront, imbues the book with a gritty realism, a vividness and authenticity that testify to the author's extensive historical research. But Rash also dignifies these workers by individualizing them through features of dress and speech and physical actions, as well as through their specific ideas and concerns. From the philosophical Snipes in his parti-color apparel to the illiterate lay preacher McIntyre, from McIntyre's gullible parishioner Stewart to the cynical, argumentative Ross and the impressionable Dunbar, the crew's youngest member at nineteen, the loggers are portrayed as singular individuals. Rash introduces this chorus briefly in chapter 2, then devotes almost all of chapter 5 to dialogue among these members of Snipes's crew, who notably discuss, given the greed of the Pembertons, the reality and value of invisible things such as love and courage and air. As Snipes, who has initiated this line of thought, states, "there is a lot more to this old world than meets the eye" (66). Yet Rash undercuts the portentousness of such exchanges by injecting them with humor, as when Stewart adds chiggers to this inventory of invisible things or Ross says, on a rainy day, "I got enough mud daubed on my ass to grow a peck of corn" (176).

Throughout the book this chorus (with McIntyre later replaced by Henryson and Dunbar killed by a falling limb) comments on the principal characters' words and actions, conveys information about violence that occurs offstage, raises assorted philosophical and religious issues, and serves as one of the novel's centers of moral conscience. The loggers also reflect on their own mortality amid the high incidence of fatal accidents to which their labors consign them. As Ross remarks, "I expect before long they'll be fittin' us for coffins ahead of time" (246). The crew links Galloway to the devil, and Dunbar remembers hearing how Galloway's severed left hand, lopped off accidentally by an inexperienced logger, "kept opening and closing like it was trying to strangle somebody" (186). Though superstitious, the crew often judges accurately, and thus their dialogue becomes one of the many devices of foreshadowing that Rash employs so effectively in *Serena*. The newspaper articles Rash has Snipes share with the crew contribute to the book's economy of presentation by enabling Rash to center much of the book's dramatic action in the camp itself while incorporating events taking place elsewhere, including Dr. Cheney's horrific mutilation and death following Serena's miscarriage.

Perhaps the most thematically significant of these choral interludes occurs in chapter 25 when, during a break from work on a rainy day, Henryson asks if Stewart has dry rolling papers for a cigarette. Stewart, who is reading his Bible, shakes his head no, whereupon Ross suggests that Stewart remove a few pages from the Bible, a proposal Stewart considers sacrilegious. In the ensuing seriocomic debate, Henryson contends that such generosity is "exactly the Christian thing to do" (248). When Snipes is called upon to resolve the dispute, he states, "Your leading scholars has argued for years you'll find cause to do or not do most anything in that book, so I'm of a mind you got to pluck out the verse what trumps the rest of them" to reach a decision, a verse Henryson then identifies as "love thy neighbor" (248). After some reflection Stewart extracts two pages from Genesis, choosing from among the "begats." The compression and humor and profound moral and religious implications of this scene, especially juxtaposed to the Pembertons' viciousness, testify both to Rash's literary artistry and to the underlying theological dimension of his thought. Serena, in contrast to Snipes's crew, dismisses al-truism as "invariably a means to conceal one's personal failures" (136) and tells Pemberton, "others can make us vulnerable," an attitude that impels the couple into increasing isolation and Serena into intensifying violence (249).

The chorus makes its final appearance in chapter 35, which consists almost entirely of dialogue and includes observations on the fate of Sheriff McDowell, tortured and murdered by Galloway. In this episode the crew comments on the countryside's polluted streams and vanished wildlife, ac-knowledging their own complicity in this destruction of nature yet noting the economic imperatives that led them into logging. This scene achieves much of its resonance because in it Preacher McIntyre, recently rehired, finally regains his powers of speech after falling silent for months following his traumatic encounter with a huge rattlesnake dropped by Serena's eagle. Asked his opinion of the devastation that surrounds the crew, McIntyre unexpectedly replies: "I think," he says, "this is what the end of the world will be like," a remark to which the narrator adds, "and none among them raised his voice to disagree" (336). In its portrait of environmental catastrophe, Serena takes its place among such works as Cormac McCarthy's The Road and Ann Pan-cake's Strange as This Weather Has Been, both novels of apocalyptic natural disasters set partially or wholly in Appalachia.[15]

Rash's portrait of Snipes's crew as chorus grounds this novel in the thoughts, emotions, and actions of working-class people who counterbal-ance the extremes of character and action manifest by the Pembertons and Galloway. The loggers are perceptive, practical, inquisitive, and sympathetic toward others. They exhibit strong senses of humor and are capable of self-criticism, traits largely absent from the Pembertons. Throughout the book their down-to-earth sanity contrasts sharply with what even the drunken Pemberton recognizes as "madness" when Serena claims that the couple is "closer than we've ever been before" because they are both murderers (278). The chorus of loggers helps to illustrate Rash's belief that Appalachia and Appalachians have much to teach those from outside the region.

Just as Rash uses the chorus to pronounce judgment on the Pembertons and Galloway, so he has Reverend Bolick denounce Pemberton and his part-ner, Harris, at the camp's church service described in chapter 17. During that service a choir sings the hymn "Thy Might Set Fast the Mountains," based on Psalms 65:6–13, verses that emphasize nature's grandeur and fertility and thus implicitly condemn both the sacrilege effected by the lumber company and the impiety of Serena and Pemberton. In fact several of the novel's most dramatic murders occur on Sunday—Abe Harmon's, Buchanan's, and that of Pemberton himself—as if to underscore the Pembertons' utter disregard for God, whose creation they ravage. For Pemberton and Harris, religion is viewed as "a great business investment," one that keeps their workers content, presumably by promising compensation in the afterlife for whatever misery and injustice they experience in the temporal world (170). Seeing Pemberton at this service, Bolick quotes the Old Testament prophet Obadiah: "The pride of thine heart hath deceived thee, . . . that saith in his heart, who shall bring me down?" (171).[16] The next verse in this shortest book of the Old Testament (just twenty-one verses long) reads, "Though you soar aloft like the eagle, though your nest is set among the stars, thence I will bring you down, says the Lord." Other verses help to foreshadow Pemberton's fate at Serena's and Galloway's hands. Verse 7, for instance, includes the statements, "All your allies have deceived you, . . . your trusted friends have set a trap for you." This retribution awaits "for the violence done to your brother Jacob," and its condemnation applies to Serena as well, as the novel's coda reveals: "As you have done, it shall be done to you, your deeds shall return on your own head" (vv. 10, 15). Reverend Bolick's reference to Obadiah thus becomes a key element in the novel's moral and religious structure amid the carnage that fills the book.

One of the final victims of that violence, other than Pemberton and Serena themselves, is Sheriff McDowell, whose incorruptibility provides another important contrast to the savage immorality of the Pembertons. Yet, ironically, the sheriff himself is forced to resort to extrajudicial action when that couple has him replaced—on trumped-up charges of malfeasance—by the aptly named Bowden, who bows to the Pembertons' will (just as Campbell, another person of integrity, is replaced by someone named Meeks). Though McDowell fails to kill the Pembertons when he burns their cabin in chapter 32, he succeeds in saving Rachel and Jacob from Galloway and enabling them to reach safety in Seattle. Not until the novel's final chapter, as Galloway oversees Pemberton's death, does the reader learn some of the details of McDowell's grisly death at Galloway's hands, a death that earns Galloway's grudging respect: "If I had it to do over," he says, "I'd as lief have killed him quick" (364). In fact Galloway later ignores Serena's wishes by refusing to grant Pemberton an easy death because, he claims, in one of the novel's most ironic passages, "It'd lay too heavy on my conscience" after the way he tortured McDowell (364). The very notion of Galloway's having a conscience will strike most readers as absurd.

Irony is one of the most prominent literary devices throughout this book, as in much of Rash's work, whether verbal irony, irony of character and incident, or dramatic irony. Serena's name is a notable instance of such irony, for she is anything but serene. Another prime example, as already mentioned, involves the bowie knife Serena returns to Rachel in the novel's opening scene only to have it become the weapon that kills her nearly half a century later. Similarly the first words readers hear from Serena in chapter 1 occur in response to Pemberton's comment that a logging camp is "not the best place for a honeymoon," to which Serena replies: "It suits us well enough. . . . We're here together, which is all that matters" (4). By novel's end, however, that *us* has been annulled when Serena plots her husband's death.

Ironies likewise abound in the chapters leading up to Pemberton's death, for although he realizes, as noted earlier, that Serena is capable of anything, he does not suspect her of planning his own murder, not even when she enlists Galloway's blind mother, who reputedly can foresee the future, as "amusement" at Pemberton's thirtieth birthday party and instructs her husband to ask the old woman "how you'll die" (343). Like the witches in *Macbeth*, Mrs. Galloway produces an ambiguous prophecy that misleads Pemberton. "They ain't one thing can kill a man like you," she predicts (344). The next day, while hunting the elusive mountain lion that Galloway has supposedly located, Pemberton finds himself dying of multiple causes: the poisoned sandwich that Serena has prepared and the rattlesnake bites he incurs while climbing onto a ledge to which Galloway directs him, among other less serious injuries. Yet even after Galloway explains why Serena wants her husband dead, Pemberton irrationally envisions rescue and reconciliation, "a new beginning" (367). Moreover, as he gazes toward the Smokies and the projected national park there, he reconfirms the predatory stance he and Serena have adopted throughout the book by wondering "how many millions of board feet of timber were in those mountains" (366).

At other times, however, Rash clearly differentiates Pemberton from Serena. While Serena herself is devoid of moral conscience and appears to believe her actions immune from negative consequences, Rash reveals through the book's other characters, including Pemberton, the importance of moral choices and of acts of generosity and love. Knowing that Rachel and Jacob are being hidden at Kephart's cabin, for instance, Pemberton contemplates killing them—but refrains from doing so. Nor does he disclose their hiding place to Serena or Galloway. His silence aids their escape, as does the money he sends them through McDowell. Moreover, despite his sense that Serena has cast a spell over him, Pemberton does not attempt to excuse himself or to see himself as a victim of overpowering circumstances. Instead he thinks of his "self-willed amnesia, a spell willingly succumbed to" and envisions himself "falling slow and deliberate and with his eyes open" (261). Similarly, in recalling his first meeting with Serena in Boston and the warning about her he had been given, he remembers hesitating at the door of her lodging: "Then he'd stepped inside, stepping toward this room as well, into this moment" (278). Whereas Serena ignores the past, Pemberton realizes the interconnections among past, present, and future. Yet against his better judgment and his repeated wish that the couple's present success "be enough" (261), he surrenders to Serena's limitless ambition when he boasts near novel's end, "Give us a lifetime and Mrs. Pemberton and I will cut down every tree, not just in Brazil but in the world" (346), a statement that recalls the novel's epigraph in its use of the term *world*.

Ultimately, then, both Pembertons ignore moral categories and any evaluative measures beyond monetary gain in assessing their actions. Their holdings in Haywood County having been clear-cut prior to the company's move to Jackson County, Serena declares, as chapter 33 closes, "We've done well here," a sentiment echoed by her husband on the day he dies when the couple has a photograph of them taken against the backdrop of "the decimated valley," a photograph that Pemberton refers to, unwittingly, as "a last birthday present" for him (351, 352). Although the photographer proposes a less dreary setting, Pemberton insists it is fine: "As Mrs. Pemberton says, we're pleased with what we've done here" (353). In the book's italicized coda, when that photograph appears in a 1975 *Life* article about Serena's "long career as a timber baroness in Brazil," she again affirms that there is nothing she has done which she regrets, "absolutely not" (369). Ironically, it is Rachel's discovery of that article and her sharing it with Jacob that leads to Jacob's killing of Serena and Galloway in October of that year, the month of Pemberton's death.

Rash's careful interweaving of such details heightens the novel's impact on readers. *Serena* demonstrates the destructive role that extractive industries have played—and continue to play—in Appalachia, but the book also offers powerful portraits of both moral bankruptcy and moral integrity. The novel speaks simultaneously to contemporary environmental concerns and to timeless issues of good and evil. Rash's attempt to link Serena to the Nazis, however, by way of the West German tractor company mentioned in the coda, a company operated by Joseph Mengele, seems forced and superfluous.[17] More effective is his allusion to Euripedes's *Medea*, which appears in the book's opening chapter when Serena quotes from that Greek play without identifying her source: "Myself will grip the sword—yea, though I die" (18). Medea's capacity for violence, which extends to her willingness to slay her own children to avenge herself on Jason, anticipates Serena's savagery. But that horror is counterbalanced by Rachel's profound love for Jacob, by the compassionate acts of those who assist her and her child, and by the moral insight, good-natured humor, and simple humaneness of Snipes's crew.

Given the level of excellence Rash achieved in *Serena*, it is hardly surprising that reviewers of his fifth novel, *The Cove*, often compared it unfavorably to its predecessor.[18] The later novel is, indeed, a lesser achievement, especially in its original hardbound edition, as Rash himself recognized in taking the unusual step of revising the book substantially before its publication in paperback in November 2012. Reviewers found the character Chauncey Feith, a World War I military recruiter, disappointingly one-dimensional, an assessment Rash apparently shared, because the paperback printing omitted two of the chapters originally devoted to Chauncey, moved another to a later position, and deleted several additional paragraphs pertaining to him.[19] Rash made more than a dozen other changes, sometimes to eliminate an anachronism, sometimes to correct an error, at other times to omit a repetitious word or sentence. Readers of *The Cove* should be aware, then, that the paperback edition must be considered definitive as the author's preferred version.

Like *Serena*, *The Cove* is set in the past, in this case during the final months of World War I, August to November 1918. Yet as in *Serena* Rash uses the past to explore contemporary issues: U.S. militarism, xenophobia, the nature of patriotism, and the irrationality that too often plagues American politics. The book's plot is partially based on the little-known internment of more than two thousand "enemy aliens" at Hot Springs, North Carolina, in Madison County—among them some fifty personnel from the German ship *Vaterland*, which had been compelled to remain in port in New York City at the outbreak of the war, these members of its crew formally interned when the United States entered the conflict in 1917.[20] Rash combines this historical material with an account of a brother and sister, Hank and Laurel Shelton, who are viewed with suspicion by many other residents of the county because Laurel bears a birthmark that leads some people to consider her a witch and because their family purchased farmland in an enclosed valley (the cove of the book's title) believed to be cursed. In his fiction and poetry, Rash regularly incorporates Appalachian folklore and superstitions, treating them respectfully and often using them to intensify a sense of mystery and wonder. In this book, however, he seems to equate people's assumptions about Laurel's being a witch with other mass delusions in the sociopolitical realm.

Rash opens this novel with a brief but engaging italicized prologue set in 1953, some thirty-five years after the narrative's principal events, when a Tennessee Valley Authority employee visits the Shelton farm prior to the projected flooding of the cove, another of many such scenes of erasure in Rash's work. Originally from Kansas, that TVA worker condescends to the local people, from whom he expects at best "*a brooding fatalism.*"[21] On this occasion, however, he discovers that there is no one to evict and that the area's nearby residents welcome the cove's inundation. "*You can't bury that cove deep enough for me, an older man named Parton said. . . . Parton muttered that the cove was a place where only bad things happened*" (1). Only later do readers learn that to win a bet Parton had persuaded the vulnerable Laurel to have sex with him and that he participated in the event that led to the deaths of Laurel and Hank. Rash uses this prologue to create an atmosphere of foreboding through such details of setting as the enormous cliff that casts the cove in deep shadow even at midafternoon and the bottle- and tin-covered ash tree that guards the path into the cove, with salt scattered below the tree to ward off witches, as with the salt Amy carries when visiting the Widow Glendower in *One Foot in Eden.* Despite an ornithologist's claim that the cove "*might hold the last Carolina Parakeets in the world,*" the TVA employee "*couldn't imagine anything that bright and colorful ever being here,*" so bleak does the cove appear to him (3). Rash also uses this prologue to shift the novel in the direction of a murder mystery, as he had in *One Foot in Eden,* for at the Shelton farm the TVA worker sees two wells, only one with a pulley. When he lowers the bucket on that pulley for a drink, he draws up a human skull.

Compared to *Serena, The Cove* has a relatively small cast of characters: Hank and Laurel, their elderly neighbor Slidell, an escaped German internee named Walter, Chauncey Feith, and assorted residents in and near Mars Hill, an actual town in Madison County with a college named after it, the Shelton farm lying three miles away. The place-name Mars Hill, with its reference to the Roman god of war, is appropriate to the book's timeframe and subject matter, with one reviewer terming *The Cove* a "powerful anti-war novel."[22] While that claim seems hyperbolic, the book compellingly conveys the pain and suffering war causes, not only for Hank, a conscript who has lost his left hand and lower arm in France, but also for characters such as Paul Clayton, gassed in the trenches, his lungs seared, and Tillman Estep, who loses an eye and has his face horribly disfigured by shrapnel. "Even in a war, you'd think some things wouldn't be allowed," says one of Paul's uncles (89). Amid the United States' ongoing war in Afghanistan and its recently concluded war in Iraq, with all the fatal and maiming injuries sustained by combatants and civilians alike, *The Cove* documents some of the human costs of such violence.

Those costs include not just physical deaths and injuries but emotional and spiritual wounds, as supposed enemies are demonized and irrational hatred and fear displace love and empathy. Rash, like Francisco de Goya, assumes that the sleep of reason—and the numbing of the heart—breeds monsters, or at the very least a terrifying irrationality. As the college's persecuted German professor states, quoting from Caesar's *Gallic War, Libenter homines id quad volunt credunt:* "Men are glad to believe that which they wish for" (156).[23] Moreover readers of Rash's third novel, *The World Made Straight,* may find in Laurel's name, as well as in the Madison County setting of *The Cove,* a reminder of bloody Madison's most infamous Civil War atrocity, the Shelton Laurel massacre, especially when Slidell in *The Cove* recalls the deaths of his father and sixteen-year-old brother, shot by outliers for being "Lincolnites," Union sympathizers (81). Like *The World Made Straight* and several of Rash's best short stories, *The Cove* reveals war to be among the author's most obsessive subjects.

This historical-political dimension of the book is counterpointed, however, by the love story Rash tells involving Laurel and Walter, a plot element foreshadowed in the novel's epigraph, the opening lines of stanza 34 of John Keats's poem "The Eve of St. Agnes." Rash builds sympathy for Laurel because she is the sibling most deeply affected by the community's superstition and intolerance and because she is left alone while Hank serves overseas.[24] A young woman in her late twenties, Laurel is still "waiting for her life to begin," and she sees Walter's arrival as offering an alternative to her terrible isolation, especially with Hank soon to be married (47). Walter escapes from internment in August 1918, as one of the Germans at Hot Springs actually did the preceding year.[25] A former musician in the orchestra aboard the *Vaterland,* the world's largest ship at the time it was seized by the United States and later transformed into the USS *Leviathan,* Walter is playing his flute when Laurel first notices him hiding in the woods. Pretending to be mute, he carries a note explaining his physical disability and expressing his wish to travel by train to New York. Thus begins their quickly deepening relationship.

Walter's identity as a musician allows Rash to comment at various points on the nature and function of art, including the literary arts. In a novel that critiques humanity's credulity, intolerance, and cruel indifference to the well-being of others, Rash portrays art as engendering empathy and a sense of human interconnection. According to Laurel, "just hearing music, even the saddest sort of song, lets you know you're not all of every way alone, that someone else has known the likesomeness of what you have" (53). On another occasion, as Walter and Slidell play flute and guitar together, Laurel remarks, "There's a blessingness in the having heard it" (92). For Laurel, Walter's music makes the cabin "less gloamy, as though the music pulled in more light through the windows and chink gaps" (54). Art's capacity to enlighten, to dispel darkness of heart and mind and spirit, is an article of faith for Rash, one particularly pertinent to a novel that addresses irrational prejudices, fears, and hatreds. Rash stresses the interpersonal bonds established by storytelling through Walter's detailed accounts of the ship's various decks, descriptions that Laurel soon masters so that his story and hers merge, "and this place [the cove]," she says, "can't lay claim on me any more" (170). Her statement reflects the power of art to liberate, to enable people to transcend, through the literary or artistic imagination, their time and place and circumstances.

In one of the novel's key satiric episodes, it is precisely this transformative power of art, specifically of books, that Chauncey Feith finds so objectionable—enough so that he invades the college's library looking for books in German, convinced that they are seditious. Unable to read that language, Chauncey has seized a book from Professor Mayer, whom he interrogates and browbeats, to aid in his identification of suspicious volumes. That book turns out to be a translation of Whitman's poems, with Rash quoting in German a portion of section 51 of "Song of Myself," lines that in their original English emphasize the American poet's—and America's—inclusiveness: "Do I contradict myself? / Very well then, I contradict myself, / (I am large, I contain multitudes)" (140).[26] The other passage Rash quotes in this episode comes from the German poet Heinrich Heine, who in his 1821 play *Almansor* wrote, "*Das war ein Vorspiel nur, dort wo man Bücher / verbrennt, verbrennt man auch am Ende Menschen,*" lines that can be translated, "That was only a prelude; there where someone burns books, he also in the end burns people," a quotation that eerily anticipates the Holocaust (140). Chauncey tightly circumscribes, along hyperpatriotic lines, the breadth of his sympathies. For Chauncey the very German language "looked sinister, especially the two dots [the German umlaut] that resembled a rattlesnake bite" (141). He thus rejects the liberating force that art offers, preferring instead his provincial, chauvinistic, egocentric outlook. Though somewhat heavy-handed, Rash's portrait of Chauncey in this scene captures the virulent anti-German sentiment that swept much of the United States during World War I.

At several key points in this novel, Rash makes reference to Carolina parakeets, a leitmotif in *The Cove* similar to the one involving mountain lions in *Serena,* not only to raise environmental concerns but also to limn an alternative to Chauncey's narrowly delimited sense of community. Rash foregrounds this motif by referring to that bird in both the prologue and in the first chapter's opening paragraph, as well as by placing a woodcut of the parakeet on the book's title page and at the beginning of each of its five numbered sections. Laurel recalls her elementary school teacher's circulating a dead Carolina parakeet among the members of her class and mentioning the species' imminent extinction. When a classmate remarks on the birds' stupidity because they keep circling rather than fleeing after other members of the flock are shot, the teacher explains, "It's not because they're stupid. . . . They never desert the flock" (9). The birds' cry of *we we we* can be seen to give voice to this sense of solidarity, exhibited again in Laurel's memory of their slaughter by her now-dead parents. Rash later contrasts these birds' mutual support with the behavior of the biddies Laurel recalls attacking an injured baby chick and killing it.

Upon first hearing Walter's flute, Laurel wonders whether she is hearing a Carolina parakeet. And when she finds Walter barely conscious after being severely stung by yellow jackets, she demonstrates the concern for others that the parakeets symbolize by caring for the injured man, Rash seeming to draw on the parable of the Good Samaritan as well. While Hank initially begrudges the aid his sister expects him to provide Walter, for Laurel the situation is clear: "We know he's hurt, . . . and we know there's not another near to help him" (40). Rash indicates Laurel's naïveté, however, by having her think, "she didn't believe anyone who made such beautiful sounds could be dangerous" (51). In Rash's work beauty and goodness do not necessarily coincide, as he shows in *Serena* when Pemberton applies Lord Byron's poem "She Walks in Beauty" to Serena, even though Byron depicts the woman's beauty as "tell[ing] of days in goodness spent, / A mind at peace with all below."[27]

Through his portrait of Chauncey, Rash also takes note of the potential danger of narrowly defined conceptions of solidarity, with the hatred they can engender for those outside one's group. In "A Note on the Revisions to This Edition" that appeared in the novel's paperback reprinting, the author explains that he "returned to an earlier version of the novel, one which focuses much more, to use Robert Frost's adage, on grief not grievances. Thus this version deepens the focus on Laurel, Hank, and Walter, while returning Chauncey Feith to minor character status." "Should readers wish for more of Chauncey," he adds, "they need only close the book and look around." Rash's specific grievances arose from the actions of the Bush administration and especially Vice President Dick Cheney, actions that led the United States into a war in Iraq based on allegations, later proven false, that Saddam Hussein possessed weapons of mass destruction. Members of Congress endorsed that war, committing thousands of Americans to combat with little risk to themselves. Feith, too, remains insulated from combat while inducing others to enlist and establishing a Boys Working Reserve corps to inculcate his brand of patriotism. Himself a child of privilege whose father is a banker, the self-important Chauncey names his horse Traveler after Gen. Robert E. Lee's famous mount. Attempting to compensate for his own shortcomings, he plans an elaborate welcome-home celebration for Paul Clayton, a former member of the Boys Working Reserve whom Chauncey persuaded to enlist. And in his paranoia about Madison County's being "overrun with Germans" (63), he initiates a petition to the president of Mars Hill College demanding that its German professor be fired and banned from campus and that the college's librarian be "at the very least, severely reprimanded" for allowing "potentially subversive books in the campus library" (118). Chauncey's xenophobia finds its counterpart both in the anti-German sentiment of his era and in the anti-Muslim and anti-immigrant rhetoric of early twenty-first-century America.

Not surprisingly it is Chauncey who commits the needless, fatal violence with which *The Cove* concludes. Much of the book traces the developing love affair between Laurel and Walter after Walter is persuaded to remain in the cove to help Hank on the farm, his one attempt to leave for New York stymied when he sees a wanted poster of himself at the local train depot. Eventually realizing that Walter can indeed talk and having learned his identity, Laurel is eager to leave with him as soon as the war ends. Given the novel's epigraph, readers familiar with Keats's "Eve of St. Agnes" might expect Laurel and Walter, like Keats's lovers, to make their escape. But grimmer outcomes typically befall Rash's characters. On the day of Paul Clayton's homecoming, Paul's uncles see the wanted poster at the train depot and recognize Walter from an earlier encounter with him, a discovery reported to Chauncey, who leads a group of men and some of the boys from his Working Reserve to the Shelton farm, declaring, "We're arresting them all. . . . What's the truth and what ain't we can sort out later" (213). In the ensuing action, these vigilantes tie Hank to his porch post and then enter the woods in search of Walter and Laurel, and Laurel is fatally shot by Chauncey when the pistol he has pointed at her accidentally discharges. Returning alone to Hank, Chauncey kills the defenseless man to prevent Hank from avenging Laurel's death. Afterward, seeing Slidell approach the Sheltons' cabin, Chauncey tries to slip away—only to fall, unobserved, into the old well from which the TVA employee recovers a skull in the novel's prologue.

So dark an ending, common in Rash's fiction, may seem to confirm the cove's reputation as a place accursed. As the book's title indicates, setting is a major feature of this book's artistry and design. However optimistic Laurel

and Hank at times become, as when she feels as if "some benevolent spell
. . . had been cast over the cabin" with Walter's arrival, at the time she anticipates leaving the cove forever, her attitude toward it is primarily negative
(135). She looks forward to being completely "shed of this place and its ever-
always miserableness" (203). Yet ironically, on the day she is killed following
her picnic with Walter, she leaves a quilt and wine bottle beside the stream
for others to find, a sign "that something happy could happen here" (218).
While the light-blocking cliff casts a pall over the cove, seeming to reinforce
Rash's notion of landscape as destiny, he uses the streamside granite outcrop
on which this picnic (and an earlier one) occurs as a contrasting feature of
setting representative of light and warmth. For Laurel the outcrop resembles
"a huge hand that lifted her out of the cove's bleakness" (44). These distinctive features of setting illustrate Rash's conception of the duality of human
experience, with good and evil, joy and misery, inextricably interwoven and
thus with suffering a frequent condition of human existence in the temporal
world.

For Rash that experience of suffering appears essential to the artist,
and perhaps to all human beings, because it encourages the development of
empathy and compassion, just as people's mistreatment of Laurel nurtures
her sympathy for Walter. (This idea is also evident, as the preceding chapter
noted, in Muir's poem "One Foot in Eden," from which Rash took the title
and epigraph for his first novel.) According to Walter's mentor, Goritz, the
conductor who offers him employment in New York, it is the experience
of suffering that will give Walter the maturity to become an accomplished
musician. At novel's end, having evaded capture and death, as do Travis and
Dena in *The World Made Straight,* Walter leaves for New York, aided by the
kindhearted Slidell, who had seen the wanted poster weeks earlier but had
remained silent, realizing that Walter was no saboteur and hoping his presence would bring love to Laurel's life. Rash concludes *The Cove* with a brief
but powerful understatement presented through Walter's consciousness: "He
would tell Goritz that he was ready" (239).

For Janet Maslin "that sentence affirms Mr. Rash's reputation for writerly
miracles" in its offering of "one perfectly wrenching last thought."[28] Yet *The
Cove* disappoints in its reliance on the one-dimensional villains Chauncey
Feith and Jubel Parton and in the slow pace of its developing action, particularly in part 4, which revolves around Hank's and Walter's digging of a
new well. While that project creates some suspense because of the danger of
the work, it seems necessitated primarily by the prologue's reference to the
farm's two wells, not by the dictates of theme or characterization, although

that section's focus on water should remind readers of the eventual fate of the cove as well as of humanity's dependence on nature for this vital resource. Despite its flaws, however, *The Cove* remains what Alden Mudge calls "a haunting narrative of intolerance," a book that "dramatizes a hope that loving, reasonable sensibilities will prevail—and a fear of the tragic consequences if they do not."[29]

CHAPTER 6

Burning Bright and *Nothing Gold Can Stay*

Between 2010 and 2013, Rash published four books, two of them collections of short stories: *Burning Bright* (2010), which won the international Frank O'Connor Short Story Award, and *Nothing Gold Can Stay* (2013), which Janet Maslin in her review for the *New York Times* called Rash's "best book since his 2008 *Serena*."[1] Like *Chemistry and Other Stories,* both of these volumes demonstrate a range of characters, situations, and themes evincing the fertility of Rash's imagination. Yet the collections also reveal a clear continuity with the fictional world he has been fleshing out over the course of his career, as most of the stories are set in the mountains of western North Carolina and several draw their inspiration from poems that appeared a decade or so earlier in *Among the Believers* and *Raising the Dead.* Two of the stories are likewise linked to the novels *Saints at the River* and *The World Made Straight.* Such actual place-names as Boone and Marshall, Canton, Sylva, and Bryson City occur regularly in these stories, as does the Great Smoky Mountains National Park. The temporal settings here extend from the Civil War to the present, with both books' initial stories set in the past, as if to emphasize the crucial role consciousness of history plays in Rash's work. These stories, in their concision of language and compression of form, as well as in their focus on key dramatic incidents in the characters' lives, confirm their author's increasing mastery of this genre.

Burning Bright, dedicated to Rash's mother, consists of twelve stories divided into two numbered parts of six stories each, a symmetrical structure that may owe something to the William Blake poem "The Tyger," from which Rash takes the book's title. In Blake's poem both the opening and closing stanzas begin with the line "Tyger! Tyger! burning bright," and both stanzas conclude by referring to that animal's "fearful symmetry."[2] "The Tyger" comes from Blake's sequence *Songs of Experience* and raises questions about the power that created so fierce and potentially deadly a creature. Unlike its counterpart, "The Lamb," in Blake's *Songs of Innocence,* a poem whose second stanza answers the questions posed in the first, "The Tyger" is composed entirely of questions, ending with the query "What immortal hand or eye / Dare frame thy fearful symmetry?" Rash's choice of title for his book thus alludes to what philosophers and theologians call the problem of evil; at the same time, however, that title allows Rash to evoke more positive images and associations of fire and brightness. As a source of life-sustaining heat, fire is essential to human well-being, and the light produced by fire can bring knowledge and illumination. But fire can also be utterly destructive. The fire imagery that helps to unify this volume represents, then, the duality of human identity and experience, its capacity for both good and evil.

Evil and suffering befall many of the characters in *Burning Bright,* sometimes evil willingly embraced, sometimes evil inflicted upon them—whether by others, by economic circumstances, or by the very fact of human finitude. Two of the stories in part 1, for example, focus on the consequences of meth addiction for family members of those addicted. At times Rash details the rationalizations people use to justify morally dubious choices, as in "Dead Confederates" and "Into the Gorge." At other times he highlights the virtues of compassion and hope amid the suffering to which evil gives rise, as he does in the opening story, "Hard Times," one of the book's finest achievements.

Although set on a farm in the 1930s during the Great Depression, "Hard Times" speaks powerfully to the economic problems of the Great Recession in the twenty-first century, especially those of unemployment, foreclosure, and hunger. Inspired by Rash's earlier poem "Madison County: 1934," the story centers on an incident of egg-stealing, the thief originally believed to be a snake but turning out to be a neighbor's child.[3] Whereas the poem has just sixteen lines, the story runs to sixteen pages and covers a three-day period in the characters' lives. Shifting the setting from the poem's Madison County to Watauga County, Rash offers a chilling account of the poverty of the Hartleys as it is seen by Edna and Jacob, the owners of the henhouse. "With their ragged clothes hanging loose on bony frames," Rash writes, the Hartleys "looked like scarecrows en route to another cornfield."[4] The story is told from Jacob's third-person limited point of view, Rash contrasting his compassion with his wife's harshness and with Mr. Hartley's seeming cold-heartedness (despite the *hart* in his surname). For when Edna accuses the Hartleys' dog of stealing her eggs, Hartley calmly slits the hound's throat, not from cruelty but from pride. The following evening more eggs disappear, so Jacob inserts a fishhook into an egg, tying fishing line to the hook to catch the snake he believes is the culprit—only to find Hartley's eight- or nine-year-old daughter in the henhouse with the hook embedded in her cheek. Jacob removes the hook, treats the girl's wound, and allows her to eat the other egg she still clutches. Even though he forbids her to return, he does not report her to either her father or to Edna, telling his wife, "It was a snake" (17).

In the story's closing paragraph, Rash creates a visionary moment for Jacob—a motif that recurs in several of the book's stories—but one not marked by Jacob's customary hopefulness. "Instead," Rash states, "he imagined towns where hungry men hung on boxcars looking for work that couldn't be found, shacks where families lived who didn't even have one swaybacked milk cow. He imagined cities where blood stained the sidewalks beneath buildings tall as ridges. He tried to imagine a place worse than where he was" (18). There is no sentimentalizing of Appalachia or of the agrarian past in this story. The note on which "Hard Times" concludes is grim indeed, but that grimness is relieved, at least in part, by Jacob's display of compassion.

The second and fourth stories in part 1, "Back of Beyond" and "The Ascent," deal with meth addiction, which has reached epidemic proportions in contemporary Appalachia but which is scarcely a regional problem alone; rather it has parallels to drug abuse in other parts of the United States and the world. In both these stories, normal family relationships are disrupted by drug use. In "Back of Beyond," a title that suggests an extremely remote physical setting, Rash places the characters in Jackson County, one of the counties logged in *Serena*. The protagonist, Parson, having grown up on a family farm he has gladly left, now lives in Tuckasegee, where he runs a pawnshop, his principal customers the area's meth addicts. Rash paints a devastating portrait of the physical damage done by meth: "When the woman spoke Parson glimpsed the stubbed brown ruin inside her mouth" (21). Parson also recognizes the addicts by the odor accompanying them, "a sour ammonia smell like cat piss" (22). Rash sets this story, appropriately, in winter, as he does "The Ascent," with snow falling in both narratives to symbolize the numbing effect of addiction and its consequent severing of human ties. But Parson, unlike the child protagonist of "The Ascent," is not a victim of meth addicts; instead he profits from their woes, even purchasing an antique clock and other household items from his nephew Danny, another addict. Parson is estranged from Danny's father (his brother Ray), whom he has not visited at the family homestead in nearly a year and where he has not stayed overnight in nearly forty years. In addition Parson is divorced from his wife, who has told him, "You can't feel love. . . . It's like you were given a shot years ago and inoculated" (31). Rash makes it clear, then, that this protagonist is seriously flawed.

Yet when Danny sells Parson a shotgun he has stolen and the local sheriff comes to the pawnshop to recover the weapon, Parson goes to the family farm both to warn Danny and to recoup the twenty dollars paid for the gun. There he finds Danny's parents living—without electricity and with almost no food—in their son's frigid trailer, to which they have retreated to avoid Danny and his friends. To support his addiction, Danny has not only been stealing but has also been cashing his parents' social security checks. His mother, moreover, is an enabler, repeatedly asserting to Parson, "It ain't his fault" (29, 31). For a moment Parson considers burning Danny out of the family's home, but instead he drives Danny and his girlfriend to Sylva, where he buys them one-way bus tickets to Atlanta. Returning to the farm, Parson moves Ray and Martha back into their house, builds a warm fire, and feeds them. Even though that fire evokes an archetypal experience, with Parson recalling "how ten thousand years ago people would have done the same thing on a cold night," Martha resents Parson's interference, and Ray simply seems baffled by the upheaval in their lives (41). Nor, despite his rescue of Ray and Martha, does Parson appear to alter significantly as a result of this experience, for in the story's closing sentence he anticipates another day at his pawnshop: "Whatever time he showed up, they'd [the addicts] still be there" (43). The single-day time frame Rash uses in the story intensifies the dramatic action but does not mark a turning point in Parson's life. He will continue to benefit from others' addiction.

Whereas Danny exploits his parents, Jared, the fifth-grade protagonist of "The Ascent," in a striking role reversal, becomes the caregiver for his meth-addicted father and mother, whose addiction reduces them to child-like dependency. Rash builds the story around an actual event, the crash of a couple's small plane in the mountains of western North Carolina. Set close to and inside the Great Smoky Mountains National Park during Jared's Christmas vacation, "The Ascent" has the boy discover the plane, to which he makes three trips over the course of the story. On the first occasion he takes a ring from the dead woman's hand, planning to give it to his classmate Lyndee. When the boy's father sees the ring, however, he confiscates it and sells it to purchase more drugs, although he has enough love for Jared to spend some of the money on his son's favorite cereal and on a used mountain bike intended as a Christmas gift. Once that supply of meth has been consumed and the parents again suffer withdrawal symptoms, Jared returns to the plane, where he removes the dead husband's watch, a Rolex, which his parents promptly take to Bryson City to sell. In their absence Jared revisits the plane, taking tools with him to repair the plane for the ascent mentioned in the story's title. Preferring this literally dead couple to his death-in-life parents, Jared envisions the plane soaring above the snow-laden landscape as he succumbs to the cold and to death.

As in "Back of Beyond," so in "The Ascent" Rash uses hearth and fire imagery to underscore the ironic breakdown of the Celtic "bonding fire" he celebrates in *Saints at the River* and in a poem of that title in *Waking*. After Jared's first trip to the plane, Rash describes the grotesque sight that greets the boy upon his return home: "His father kneeled before the fireplace, meticulously arranging and rearranging kindling around an oak log. A dozen crushed beer cans lay amid the kindling, balanced on the log itself three red-and-white fishing bobbers. . . . 'It's going to be our Christmas tree,'" announces Jared's mother, adding strips of tinfoil to the log (79). That evening when the fire is lit, "the foil and cans withered and blackened, the fishing bobbers melting," an apt image of the dissolution of Jared's parents' lives and of his family's bonds. No bright burning redeems Jared's situation, only the fire of his imagination's projected ascent, which will ultimately leave him as earthbound as his parents' temporary highs do them. Rash vividly depicts the horrible impact of drug addiction on traditional family life.

Between these two tales of addiction, Rash places the delightfully comedic "Dead Confederates," one of the book's three first-person narratives. But the comedy sometimes veers toward black humor in this story of greed, grave robbing, and sudden death set in Madison County, the scene of the Shelton Laurel massacre. Rash immediately gains the reader's attention in the narrator's opening sentence: "I never cared for Wesley Davidson when he was alive and seeing him beside me laid out dead didn't much change that" (45). In addition to Wesley and the unnamed narrator, the only other major character is the elderly caretaker of the cemetery in which Wesley and the narrator excavate two graves in search of valuable Confederate artifacts: belt buckles, buttons from military uniforms, and swords. It is Wesley who proposes this gruesome enterprise to the narrator, who is facing pressing medical bills from his mother's hospitalization and trying to prevent the bank from repossessing his truck.

In this tale's retrospective structure and in the narrator's closing nightmare about being buried alive, "Dead Confederates" is indebted, it would seem, to Edgar Allan Poe's "The Cask of Amontillado." Although most of the story is told in present tense, lending the action immediacy, the final paragraph reveals that these events occurred a year earlier. Rash generates sympathy for his working-class narrator, who rationalizes his participation in Wesley's scheme, by portraying Wesley as a one-dimensional villain: lazy, self-serving, hypocritical, and deceitful. Weighing some three hundred pounds, the out-of-shape Wesley obviously needs the narrator to disinter the Confederate coffins. When the narrator insists that Wesley help dig up the second grave, that of a Lieutenant Hutchinson buried in 1864, Rash foreshadows Wesley's death by describing the "veins sticking out on his neck like there's a noose around it" (59). During this second disinterment, the two men are discovered by the caretaker, whom Wesley tries to bribe and to whom he lies. The caretaker lets them proceed because his ancestors "sided Union" and because the dead officer served with the North Carolina Sixty-Fourth Regiment, the unit responsible for whipping the caretaker's great-grandmother to obtain information about some of the men and boys later murdered at Shelton Laurel.[5] Rash thus uses this predominantly humorous tale to remind his readers once again of the deeply divided loyalties in the mountain South during the Civil War.

After Wesley collapses and dies following the opening of the second coffin, the caretaker proposes that the narrator leave Wesley's body in that grave, a suggestion to which the narrator assents. "You shouldn't get the fantods over this," says the caretaker, using a term most readers will have encountered, if at all, only in Twain's *Adventures of Huckleberry Finn;* there it refers to the mental distress caused by delirium tremens (68).[6] The caretaker's lack of sympathy for Wesley reinforces the reader's own distancing from this character, a distancing that Rash has carefully crafted, in part by giving this story features of the tall tale. Yet the narrator's monthly nightmare of being buried alive with Wesley indicates that his conduct continues to trouble him. His earlier assumption that "I can go with Wesley just this one time, pay off that hospital bill, and be done with it" proves false (52). At story's end, however, having paid that bill, the narrator is willing to suffer this "fearsome dream . . . if it's the worst to come of all that happened" (74). Though he is not prompted by the avarice that motivates Wesley, the narrator has short-circuited his conscience, joining Wesley in actions that demonstrate their mutual immorality. Like the coffined soldiers whose graves they invade, they are—at least ethically—dead confederates. But the humorous elements here keep that moral lesson from becoming heavy-handedly didactic.

One of the comedic pleasures of this story is Rash's skillful use of vernacular speech by all three characters. The caretaker, for instance, tells Wesley, "I don't think I've heard the truth walk your lips yet," his personification of truth endowing this statement with the concreteness of the best folk speech (64). That precision of diction is evident again when the narrator says of the cast-iron coffin in which Hutchinson is buried, "That coffin *spries* Wesley up some," because its contents will be well preserved (66; italics added). The narrator describes himself "footlogging" the opened coffin to avoid stepping on its skeleton and thinks "how easy it would be for him [the caretaker] to rooster that trigger and shotgun me" (68, 71). In this tale Rash's prose has a vividness and energy that complement the exertions of the characters' activities.

The last two stories in part 1, "The Woman Who Believed in Jaguars" and "Burning Bright," like "The Ascent," present characters who are beset by a terrible loneliness, a loss (or potential loss) of family connections. The former is one of only two stories in this book set outside the North Carolina mountains, in this case in Columbia, South Carolina, and its protagonist, Ruth Lealand, is haunted by death and absence: the recent death of her mother; that many years ago of her infant son, who lived only four hours and whose death precipitated the dissolution of her marriage; and that of the now-extinct jaguars she believes once inhabited her state, as a textbook she recalls reading in third grade reported. An only child now devoid of immediate family, a woman who often "feels invisible" in her workplace, Ruth collects flyers about missing children and seeks to confirm her assumption about the jaguars (93). At stake in this story is the importance of memory in preserving the past and the dead, a theme central to Rash's poetry and fiction. Moreover this story anticipates Rash's references to Carolina parakeets in *The Cove,* for when Ruth consults the assistant director of the zoo in Columbia, he not only researches jaguars for her but also provides her with an account of these birds' loyalty to fallen members of the flock. "The affection of the survivors seemed rather to increase," he quotes from a nineteenth-century account of the birds' slaughter (105). Ruth's dream-vision in the story's closing paragraph of a jaguar-haunted tropical landscape displacing Columbia's cityscape brings relief from her sense of isolation, but whether that unburdening will be permanent or temporary remains ambiguous.

The book's title story also features a female protagonist, Marcie, whose second husband proves to be an arsonist. While the story's principal action occurs over just two days, flashbacks afford details about Marcie's first husband's death, her courtship with and second marriage to Carl, and her growing suspicions about his role in the fires plaguing the countryside near Sylva. It is Marcie, ironically, who bought Carl a cigarette lighter bearing "the image of a cloisonné tiger" on their one-night honeymoon in Gatlinburg, a gift that he selects from among other options (112). Nearly sixty years old, Marcie cannot bear the prospect of losing Carl and so lies to the sheriff who comes to question her. At story's end she resorts to prayer, although she "had not been to church in months, had not prayed for even longer than that" (123). Marcie lies in bed praying for rain, a rain that will counteract "the worst drought in a decade" and create conditions less conducive to fires (107). Carl's motives remain unknown, the act of arson an eruption of irrational evil, testimony to a profound flaw in human nature. As in Blake's "The Tyger," the origin of evil is an abiding mystery, but its effects are readily apparent in people's lives. For Rash those effects illustrate the veracity of Christianity's assessment of human nature as fallen. Yet even amid her deception of the sheriff, Marcie remains a sympathetic character because Rash's choice of third-person limited point of view helps assure that the reader understands and empathizes with her situation, which includes rejection by her daughters after she marries the younger Carl.

Like part 1, the second part of *Burning Bright* begins with a story, "Return," set in the past, in this case at the close of World War II. Rash reprints this text, with revisions, from *Casualties,* the story now dedicated to the memory of Robert Holder, the author's maternal uncle.[7] Like the book's opening and closing stories, "Return" is set in Watauga County, Rash's "spirit country." Its brief account of the successful homecoming of an unnamed soldier establishes a positive tone, as does the protagonist's anticipation of spring planting and the image of "a candle in the front window, . . . lit every night for a month, placed there for him, to guide him these last few steps" (132). In contrast to the destructive fires of the title story and to the loneliness of the characters in the preceding three stories, this candle signifies loving family ties. At the same time, however, the soldier's memories of combat—of being shot at by a Japanese sniper and then of killing his assailant—introduce a motif of violence that recurs, in various forms, in each of the subsequent stories in part 2.

Often that violence is impulsive, arising from circumstances that threaten the protagonist's sense of identity, as in the following two stories, "Into the Gorge" and "Falling Star." The former, like "The Ascent," is set near and in the Great Smoky Mountains National Park, its protagonist, sixty-eight-year-old Jesse, entering the park to harvest ginseng on land his father sold to the park service in 1959, the ginseng itself planted by that father. Jesse knows he is violating the law but needs the money selling the ginseng will bring. From Jesse's perspective Rash takes note of the changes that have altered land ownership patterns in Appalachia, not only the creation of national parks but also the building of more and more gated communities, housing affordable primarily to wealthy outsiders. Confronted by a park ranger raised in Charlotte, Jesse finds himself insulted, referred to as "too old to be much trouble," then called a fool (140, 141). Other people's "bulbs burn brighter," says the ranger, echoing the book's title (141). Angered by such disrespect,

Jesse pushes the ranger down an abandoned well the two men pass, only to discover that he is almost immediately the object of a manhunt. Although Rash maintains the reader's sympathy for Jesse, who demonstrates a capacity for self-criticism and humility that eludes the scornful ranger, the outcome of these impulsive actions is likely to prove disastrous for the elderly man. The story concludes with him hiding in the woods, awaiting "what would or would not come" on this climactic day in his life, the gorge of the title suggestive of the downward spiral he has initiated (151).

"Falling Star" is a slighter tale, but it too turns on an impulsive act of violence. A first-person narrative using present tense, this story is told by a working-class husband named Bobby who feels increasingly alienated from his wife, Lynn, after she decides to earn a community college degree. Jealous of Lynn, her books, and her teachers, Bobby goes to the college one evening while she is in class and slashes one of her car's tires and the tire of one of her professors—failing to notice the parking lot's security cameras. Though he expects Lynn to call requesting his assistance, she later returns home, her tire replaced by a security guard, who assures her that the incident has been taped, even the vandal's license plate number. After an abortive attempt to confess what he has done, Bobby surrenders to consequences he sees as inevitable, anticipating the end of his marriage. He is himself the falling star of the story's title, but he also comments on the absence of any falling star on which he might make a life-transforming wish. Among Lynn's textbooks, significantly, books that Bobby at one point considers burning, is *Astronomy Today*. Whereas Lynn is learning to name the constellations, to see connections among individual stars, Bobby's life is disintegrating, propelled toward chaos. In this story Rash again subverts stereotypes about Appalachians as uninterested in education, but he also underscores the estrangement from family that the pursuit of higher education sometimes produces. Yet despite the authenticity of Bobby's vernacular voice, his actions seem somewhat contrived, and his assumption that he has already lost Lynn is largely unfounded.

The final three stories in *Burning Bright* reconfirm the diversity of character and situation that marks Rash's short fiction. Like "The Woman Who Believed in Jaguars," "The Corpse Bird" is set outside western North Carolina, in Raleigh, the state capital, but unlike Ruth Lealand, Boyd Candler, this story's protagonist, was raised in the mountains, in Madison County. (Candler is also the surname of the Civil War-era doctor in *The World Made Straight*.) Both are stories about belief, "The Corpse Bird" inspired by a poem of the same title in *Among the Believers*, and both present a protagonist concerned about the well-being of a child. For Boyd, "the first in his family to attend college," where he earned a degree in engineering, the folk beliefs

of his ancestors still hold power, even in a Raleigh subdivision amid neighbors transplanted from the Northeast and Midwest (169). As with many of
Rash's poems, this story incorporates a folk superstition that Rash treats
with respect, however unenlightened or irrational it may seem. By setting the
story shortly before Halloween, moreover, he reminds readers of the residue
of superstition evident in that holiday, with its attenuated embrace of the
supernatural in ghosts, goblins, and witches. The corpse bird, an owl, when
heard three nights in succession, is believed to foretell someone's imminent
death. As the story opens, Boyd has already heard the bird on the two preceding nights, so when he learns his neighbors' daughter has been running a
high fever, he urges her parents to take her to the hospital, thus alarming the
family. Unable to persuade anyone to heed his concern, not even his wife,
who instead says she is making a doctor's appointment for *him*, Boyd cuts
down the tree in which the owl perches. Although others view Boyd as men-
tally ill, Rash portrays him sympathetically because Boyd acts out of selfless
concern for another and because he respects the mysterious interconnection
between humanity and nature to which this folk superstition attests. Waiting
for a policeman to handcuff him in the story's closing paragraph, Boyd looks
"like a man who's just set something free," writes Rash (180). The suspense
this story generates is heightened by Rash's limiting its action to a single day's
events, a temporal compression also evident in "Return," "Into the Gorge,"
"Falling Star," and the book's last two tales.

By concluding "The Corpse Bird" with the word *free* and focusing that
text on the prospect of death, Rash anticipates the collection's penultimate
story, "Waiting for the End of the World," a first-person narrative set in a
bar aptly named the Last Chance. Told by a misanthropic former high school
English teacher now supporting himself, in part, by playing guitar and singing in a band, this present-tense apocalyptic tale depicts a single evening at
the Last Chance, where customers "got to have [Lynyrd Skynyrd's song] 'Free
Bird' once an hour," the bar's owner, Rodney, tells Devon, the forty-year-old
narrator, "like his clientele were diabetics needing insulin" (182). This story
is the book's most allusive, drawing both on popular culture (the story's
title is that of an Elvis Costello song) and on canonical literary texts such as
W. B. Yeats's poem "The Second Coming" and Joseph Conrad's novella *Heart
of Darkness*. Filled with grotesque images and incidents, the story provides
a satirical portrait of the bar's denizens and a heartfelt, yet antic jeremiad,
its initial sentence concluding with Yeats's line, "surely some revelation is
at hand."[8] If so, that revelation documents the grim devolution of the human
species, imaged in Rodney's posting of "one of those Darwinian bumper
stickers with the fish outline and four evolving legs" (186). According to

Devon, "Rodney's drawn a speech bubble in front of the fish's mouth. *Exterminate the brutes,* the fish says," echoing Kurtz in Conrad's novella.[9] The Last Chance serves only one mixed drink, the Terminator, and Rodney views operating the bar as "a philosophical statement" (186). Devon initially shares Rodney's attitude, thinking "maybe it's time to halt all human reproduction." "Let God or evolution or whatever put us here," he adds, "start again from scratch" (183).

By story's end, however, Devon discerns in the customers "a yearning for the kind of freedom Van Zant's lyrics [in "Free Bird"] deal with, a recognition of the human need to lay their burdens down, . . . to actually feel unshackled, free and in flight" (189–90). It is music, song, and the aspiration contained in the lyrics that transport listeners beyond their current condition, affording them a type of transcendence, one of the major functions of art itself. As a musician, an artist figure, the narrator combats the forces of disintegration, of chaos and despair. Rash's elaborate closing sentence, ninety words long, reflects Devon's sense of control and his willingness to resist the anomie surrounding him. As he states in the final third of that sentence, again alluding to Yeats's poem, "whatever rough beast is asleep out there in the dark is getting its wake-up call and I'm ready and waiting for whatever it's got" (191). Unlike the bar's clientele, who leave the Last Chance "wailing and whimpering" and covering their eyes, Devon is a figure of strength who has a sense of purpose and confronts the threat of meaninglessness open-eyed (190).

Courage and resourcefulness in the presence of danger also mark Lily, the protagonist of the book's final story, "Lincolnites." The title refers to supporters of the Union during the Civil War, Rash basing this tale in part on a family story involving an ancestor who recalled a Confederate soldier raiding the family farm and leaving whistling "Dixie."[10] Like the opening stories in parts 1 and 2, "Hard Times" and "Return," respectively, "Lincolnites" is set in the past in Watauga County, but whereas "Return" is set in winter, with its protagonist anticipating spring, "Lincolnites" begins in spring, the pregnant Lily grateful for "the return of life after a hard winter" (193). Together with the prospect of the baby's birth, this springtime setting enables Rash to conclude the collection on an optimistic note. Yet like "Dead Confederates" and "Return," "Lincolnites" addresses the violence of war—specifically a murder committed by nineteen-year-old Lily to defend her farm from a marauding Confederate. In prose that is characteristically simple, direct, and understated, Rash describes Lily's killing of the Confederate with a foot-long knitting needle after he accepts her offer to trade sex for the draft horse he intends to steal. Although Lily recognizes her antagonist as "Mr. Vaughn" and recalls his giving Lily and her sister candy when he clerked at the Mast Store in Boone some years before, the characters' previous acquaintance "don't change nothing in the here and now," remarks Vaughn (198). In this scene Rash touches again upon the hostility that can pit neighbor against neighbor in wartime, in episodes of ethnic cleansing, or in instances of religious and racial animosity.

"Lincolnites" gains much of its power by focusing on a single day in Lily's life. Largely unfazed by Vaughn's death, Lily contemplates the work she plans to do the following morning, thankful that the ground is no longer frozen and that rain is falling: "Rain hard, she thought, thinking of what she'd be planting first when daylight came" (205). Like the narrator of "Waiting for the End of the World," Lily is a figure of strength, much different in that regard from the meth-addicted mother of "The Ascent" and the embittered Edna of "Hard Times." Lily is more effectual, too, than either Ruth Lealand of "The Woman Who Believed in Jaguars" or Marcie of "Burning Bright." As the only female protagonist in the six stories in part 2, she earns special attention from readers. Yet through the violence to which she is driven, Rash emphasizes the destructive impact of war, however bravely Lily responds to war's harsh demands. "Lincolnites" is among the book's best stories, no small achievement in a collection containing "Into the Gorge" and "The Ascent," both anthologized in *The Best American Short Stories* (2009, 2010), the former also awarded an O. Henry Prize. The book as a whole certainly evinces the burning bright of Rash's literary imagination.

The initial response to *Nothing Gold Can Stay* was more divided than that to *Burning Bright,* some reviewers praising its "deftly constructed worlds" and "unforgettable, beautifully crafted . . . stories" while others criticized what seemed to them the grimness, even misanthropy, pervading the book.[11] Liz Cook, for instance, though calling the volume "a gripping collection," referred to its "cycle of pessimism" and contended that "the world Rash imagines is cold, indifferent," writing as if Rash were some twenty-first-century literary naturalist.[12] Troy Jollimore was much more dismissive, charging that Rash lacks compassion for his characters and that the book's "only distinguishing character traits are negative ones" so that "the stories become gratingly predictable."[13] So disparaging a view, however, ignores the strikingly nuanced character analysis Rash often presents and overlooks the positive traits he features in many of the stories, especially in the book's final section. While Rash's poetry and fiction do frequently explore harsh situations and violent acts, the author typically creates sympathy for his characters and their plights. Yet *Nothing Gold* does contain a few stories, particularly "A Servant of History" and "A Sort of Miracle," from which such sympathy is absent.

For this collection, his fourteenth book, dedicated to Robert Morgan, Rash brought together fourteen stories, most of them previously published, including one from the prestigious *New Yorker,* one from the *Washington Post Magazine,* and two from *Southern Review.* The book is divided into three numbered parts of five, four, and five stories each. As in *Burning Bright,* these stories range in time from the Civil War era to the contemporary world, and as in the earlier volume, Rash highlights stories set in the past (over a third of the total) by placing them at the beginning of all three sections, by concluding the first section with such a story, and by having two such stories open the book's final section. Consciousness of history thus continues to be central to Rash's work, both as ongoing resource and as cautionary tale. The book's title establishes a connection to the past as resource by appropriating the title of Frost's well-known poem about change and loss in nature—and, by extension, in human life: key themes in Rash's fiction and poetry, too. The poem's sixth line reads, "So Eden sank to grief,"[14] recalling the postlapsarian world evident in Tracy's stories in Rash's first book, *The Night the New Jesus Fell to Earth,* and the reference to Eden in the title of his first novel. But Rash's simple and direct prose style and understated emotion likewise owe a debt to Frost's example, the poem's eight lines of iambic trimeter couplets containing no word of more than two syllables, its syntax also notably uncomplicated, with five complete sentences composed from a total of just forty words. Although the poem addresses nature's and humanity's evanescence and the loss of innocence, Frost's tone remains calm, the confronting of finitude offering a stance of equanimity and quiet conviction.

Several of this book's stories turn not on the loss of innocence, however, but on the loss of ignorance, as in the opening selection, "The Trusty," set near Asheville in the 1930s and first published in the *New Yorker.* Rash's careful control of third-person limited point of view here intensifies the story's multiple ironies as the author records the false assumptions and condescending attitude of Sinkler, the protagonist, toward the young mountain wife, Lucy, who deceives him and ultimately leads him to his death. Sinkler is the trusty of the title, a convict serving a five-year sentence for embezzlement who has persuaded his chain gang's guards to let him carry water to the other prisoners, an assignment that enables him to meet Lucy and her older husband, whose farm well becomes his source of water. Raised outside the mountains, in Montgomery, Alabama, Sinkler thinks disparagingly of this rural couple as "apple-knockers" and is repelled by their poverty.[15] Viewing Lucy as someone he can dupe, he attempts to seduce her to aid him in escaping the chain gang, winning her trust, he thinks, over a nearly two-week period before they flee. But alert readers will note—though perhaps only on a second reading—the clues Rash drops about Sinkler's faulty judgments, misperceptions indicated early in the story when he alters his first impression of Lucy's age from "mid-twenties" to "maybe eighteen, at most twenty" (4, 5). It is the trusty who proves gullible, while Lucy, as her name's etymology suggests, sees more clearly, more lucidly, St. Lucy being the patron saint of those with impaired vision—although Lucy proves anything but saintly, anything but the "angel" Sinkler calls her at one point (19).

"The Trusty" is a tale of ironic role reversals, of a trickster (Sinkler) deceived. When the convict brags about the amount of money he has, "enough saved to buy two [train] tickets," he gives Lucy a motive for murdering him (12). In what is perhaps the story's most ironic passage, Sinkler questions Lucy to insure that she is not someone who will develop a "bad conscience" about abetting his flight (12). Their escape route is one Lucy proposes, and she leads Sinkler on an arduous circular path through the woods, where her husband awaits with a rifle and a freshly dug grave. By telling the story through Sinkler's consciousness, Rash invites the reader to misjudge as the protagonist does, and thus the violent ending comes as a shock, yet also is utterly inexorable. Sinkler calmly capitulates to his fate, for he knows, as he acknowledges while trekking through the forest, that "without Lucy he'd be completely lost"—as he is with Lucy, ironically (22). At story's end, as Sinkler contemplates the imminent arrival of autumn, its falling leaves soon covering his grave, Rash again invokes the imagery of Frost's poem: "Then leaf subsides to leaf." In terms of narrative point of view and varieties of irony, this story is a virtuosic display of Rash's artistry.

The collection's title story, which follows "The Trusty," is one of three in this book that deal with the impact of drug abuse, a prominent subject in Rash's fiction ever since the publication of *The World Made Straight*. The gold in this case is a grisly memento of World War II, gold teeth and fillings from the mouths of Japanese soldiers, souvenirs that the elderly Mr. Ponder keeps in a pint jar. Although he had once considered burying these spoils of war, he believes "that would be getting off too easy somehow," and so he retains them as a reminder of his own and war's inhumanity (29). In part, then, this story addresses Rash's perennial theme of the horrors of war. But here that topic is subordinate to the issue of drug addiction, as the story's first-person narrator and his friend Donnie, who had painted and shingled Mr. Parson's house eight years earlier as fifteen-year-olds, plot to steal that gold to feed their prescription drug habits. One of three first-person narratives in the book, this story contrasts its unnamed narrator with Donnie, who is utterly unprincipled and who proposes to use the money obtained from selling the stolen gold to buy pills to sell to high school students. It is

Donnie who initiates the story's present-time action, including entering Mr. Ponder's home, where he discovers the old man lying dead and so steals not only the gold and the cash in Mr. Ponder's wallet but also his gold dental bridge. While this crime will apparently go unpunished, the reader knows from the story's title how quickly the thieves' profits will vanish to feed their addiction.

The other two stories that focus on drugs, "Those Who Are Dead Are Only Now Forgiven" and "The Magic Bus," appear in succession at the end of part 2 and the beginning of part 3. The former is another story of meth addiction, like "Back of Beyond" and "The Ascent" in *Burning Bright*. Set in and around Canton in Haywood County west of Asheville, this third-person narrative tells of promising high school graduates, Jody and Lauren, former lovers, who have drifted apart while Jody is away completing his first year of college. During that time Lauren becomes a meth addict and meth maker, abandoning her own plans to attend college. The story's principal action occurs on a single day, Rash beginning with the brief statement, "The Shackleford house was haunted" (127). That house, formerly a trysting place for Jody and Lauren, is now a haven for meth addicts, shackled by their drug habit, mere ghosts of themselves, the living dead of the story's title. Jody goes there in an unsuccessful attempt to rescue Lauren. Instead at story's end he elects to join her, a decision that may strike readers as inadequately motivated or excessively bleak. In part, though, Jody's loyalty to Lauren, however misguided, is prompted by his awareness of her abandonment by others, including her brother, and in part by Jody's consciousness that both his father and his sister's husband deserted their wives and children—a pattern Jody chooses not to repeat in his relationship with Lauren. But his decision is also influenced by the precariousness of his family's economic situation. Raised by a single working-class mother, Jody knows all too well "a life where checkbooks never quite balanced and repo men and pawnbrokers loomed one turn of bad luck away" (135). Moreover with three years of college ahead, he knows that he will have "more loans to pay back and, in such an uncertain economy, perhaps no job" upon graduation (141). Rash writes sensitively and movingly about the plight of working-class people in other stories in this collection, particularly "Cherokee" and "Twenty-Six Days." Nonetheless readers are likely to find Jody's final action quixotic at best, although Rash's reference to forgiveness in the tale's title may be meant to invoke the unconditional love that authentic forgiveness offers.

The third drug-related story, "The Magic Bus," takes place not in the contemporary world but in the early 1970s, though it is the atmosphere of the 1960s that suffuses Rash's musical allusions and the hippies he depicts.[16]

Against the backdrop of the Vietnam War, this story, like "Those Who Are Dead," focuses on a period of less than twenty-four hours, with its protagonist, Sabra, awakening from ignorance and innocence to the harsh realities of human nature. Almost sixteen years old and living on a Watauga County farm adjacent to the Blue Ridge Parkway, Sabra encounters a hippie couple from San Francisco whose Volkswagen bus has overheated. With the rest of her family away, she assists the couple, Thomas and Wendy, offering them supper and inviting them to stay overnight in the farm's barn, hidden from her parents. Dissatisfied with the monotony and provincialism of her life, Sabra yearns to escape. Rash sets this story two days before the Fourth of July to underscore his protagonist's desire for greater independence (148). Yet this is the tale of an incredibly naive Good Samaritan and of an equally naive—and destructive—pair of hippies, for while high on marijuana, a drug to which the couple introduces Sabra, Thomas decides to "free" the girl from her "chained" state on the farm by burning down the barn (170). Unable to extinguish the flames, Sabra can only watch as the barn is destroyed.

In this story, as in "Waiting for the End of the World" in *Burning Bright*, Rash's musical allusions deepen his character analysis. From the playful innocence of the Young Rascals' 1967 hit "Groovin'" to the pill-popping "White Rabbit" of the Jefferson Airplane's *Surrealistic Pillow* album of the same year, with its allusions to *Alice in Wonderland*, the music expresses the zanily misguided conceptions of freedom pervading the 1960s. But it is the sense of disillusionment that fills Joni Mitchell's "Both Sides Now," hummed by Wendy while Thomas dances with Sabra, that captures the story's concluding tone. The final stanza of that song ends with the words "It's life's illusions I recall. / I really don't know life at all." For Sabra, the reader hopes, her new recognition of what she does not know—and what she now does—will prove a catalyst for maturation.

Rash's satirical depiction of hippie counterculture in "The Magic Bus" is muted by the naïveté of Sabra. But in "A Servant of History" and "A Sort of Miracle," two of the four stories in part 2, his satire is hyperbolic and at times heavy-handed. The first of these, set in and near Sylva in 1922, describes James Wilson, a recent British university graduate, who thinks of himself as "a man venturing among the new world's Calibans" in coming to Appalachia to do musical research (83). Like famed musicologist Cecil Sharp, Wilson is what some mountain folk call a "song-catcher," seeking the tunes and lyrics of British ballads now thought to survive only in Appalachia among what Jack Weller called "yesterday's people."[17] Pompous, condescending, and ill-informed, Wilson is ignorant of history despite his sense of himself as its servant and preserver. Rash exaggerates the regional dialect of the person who becomes Wilson's guide, and thus when that man says, upon being asked his name, "I a go ba rafe," Wilson hears the response as Iago Barafe—"a name," he falsely assumes, "retained from Elizabethan drama" (86). Like Pemberton's partner, Wilkie, in *Serena,* who keeps a notebook containing mountain locutions of "Elizabethan" origin, Wilson overemphasizes, as some scholars have, residual Elizabethan elements in Appalachian culture. And like the Swede in Stephen Crane's "The Blue Hotel," Wilson believes that he is entering the Wild West, envisioning western North Carolina as filled with "cabins and teepees, cattle drives and saloons," and so is disappointed to find that "automobiles outnumbered horses" (84).

The lighthearted comedy and satire of the story's opening pages swerve abruptly toward a darker humor, however, when Rafe takes Wilson to meet the McDonald family, whose surname Wilson mishears as McDowell. There Wilson listens to the family's nearly one-hundred-year-old matriarch sing "The Betrothed Knight," a ballad of Rash's invention. Seeing the red-and-black tartan of the McDonald clan hanging on the wall and seeking to ingratiate himself with the family so that the old woman will sing additional ballads, Wilson mentions his Scottish ancestry on his mother's side, her maiden name being Campbell. At this news a marked chill emanates from the McDonalds, and the musicologist vaguely recalls "some connection between English kings and Argyle Campbells and . . . Clan McDonald" (93). When Granny McDonald proposes she sing "The Snows of Glencoe," Wilson suddenly remembers the seventeenth-century Glencoe massacre and his ancestors' role in it.[18] Though his mother had once told him that "it's all in the past," that past comes back to haunt him when Luther McDonald plucks a heated poker from the fireplace and burns Wilson's tongue, rejecting the money he offers to avoid harm (94). The story's closing sentence finds Wilson back in London, where he is hailed as a hero, "worthy of mention with Sir Walter Raleigh and Captain John Smith, . . . who also left their civilized isle to venture among the new world's Calibans" (96).

Rash's allusion to the Glencoe massacre of February 13, 1692, reveals, however, that Britain has not always acted "civilized." Some forty members of the McDonald clan were slain by Captain Campbell of Glenlyon on orders from Prince William, even though the McDonalds had shown hospitality to Campbell and his troops and even though the chief of the McDonalds had sworn an oath of allegiance to the prince.[19] This massacre should once again remind readers of the prominence of the Shelton Laurel massacre in Rash's fiction and poetry, as well as of his emphasis on historical consciousness. Wilson fancies himself "a servant of history" while forgetting and misrepresenting it. The repetition of the opening paragraph's phrase "the new world's

Calibans" at the end of this story implies that Wilson has learned little from his experience in Jackson County.

The humor and satire in "A Sort of Miracle" are far more outlandish. Here again the story's time frame consists of a single day, with most of the action set in winter in the Great Smoky Mountains National Park, where Denton has baited a bear trap in hopes of solving the sexual problems that have arisen between him and his wife, Susie, since her younger brothers, the oddly named Baroque and Marlboro, moved in with the couple two months earlier. Not only is bear hunting in a national park, as Denton knows, "a lot illegal," but Denton wants just the bear's paws and gall bladder, which Chinese folklore promises can cure impotence (108). Like O'Connor and Eudora Welty, Rash satirizes his characters' dependence on popular culture as their guide to living. Susie, for instance, the head nurse at the county clinic, tries vainly to induce her unemployed brothers to obtain hospital jobs by having them watch TV shows with such titles as *Medical Mysteries* and *I Survived,* "shows about hundred-pound tumors or people who'd lost all their toes to frostbite or who internally combusted" (114). Yet the characters in this story are too buffoonish to be credible.

While Rash may show little compassion for the characters in "The Trusty," "A Servant of History," and "A Sort of Miracle," in most of the book's stories he does create sympathetic characters. Part 2, for instance, also includes the poignant "Twenty-Six Days," the amount of time the first-person narrator's daughter Kerrie has remaining on her tour of duty in Afghanistan. Kerrie comes from a working-class family and appears to have enlisted to become eligible for the army's educational benefits. Her father holds two custodial jobs, one at an unnamed Appalachian college, the other in a doctor's office; her mother is a waitress. "We wouldn't be in Afghanistan if there was still a draft," says the narrator, Rash thus indicating the extent to which America's recent wars have been waged by the children of the working class and those for whom the military offers an escape from poverty, unemployment, or low wages (97). Kerrie's father thinks of the college students as unaware of or insensitive to the plight of their peers and recalls hearing someone on television say, "Just a bunch of stupid hillbillies fighting a stupid war" (98). As Rash recognizes, economic necessity, not just patriotism, has often led to a disproportionately high rate of enlistment among young people from the mountain South. But his narrator also recalls hurtful remarks by some of the college's professors, for when one teacher gives the narrator books for Kerrie, who plans to major in education upon completing her military service, another professor tells a third that her father will "just turn around and sell them, but better the flea market than the outhouse"

(100). In fact the narrator browses in one of those books, *Selected Stories of Anton Chekhov,* and is moved to tears by the Russian author's famous tale "Misery," which recounts a father's intense grief over the death of his child, grief that he is able to communicate only to his horse.

The failure of human communication and community in Chekhov's story suggests the chasm that insulates so many Americans from the violence perpetrated abroad in their country's name. Set on the day before Thanksgiving, "Twenty-Six Days" leaves Kerrie's fate unresolved, though Rash raises the possibility of her death both by alluding to Chekhov's tale and by having her parents clean up a bloodstain in the doctor's waiting room. Significantly that bloodstain results from a logger's nearly severing his arm, an injury reminiscent of the myriad accidents that befall the workers in *Serena.* This story is one of several illustrating Rash's political and economic concerns and his varied treatment of the subject of war.

Three of the stories in *Nothing Gold Can Stay,* including two in part 3, draw their inspiration from previous publications by Rash. "Something Rich and Strange" in part 1 begins with three paragraphs that reprint, with some revision, the opening italicized section of *Saints at the River.* The story's title, taken from Ariel's song in the second scene of *The Tempest,* refers to the transformation wrought by death—in Shakespeare's play the presumed drowning of Ferdinand's father, Alonso, who is later discovered alive:

> Full fathom five thy father lies;
> Of his bones are coral made;
> Those are pearls that were his eyes;
> Nothing of him that doth fade
> But doth suffer a sea change
> Into something rich and strange.[20]

The death described in Rash's story, however, has actually occurred. Yet although it is a physical fact, Rash presents it as a mysterious process, a kind of liberation, in lyrical prose that creates the fictional equivalent of a musical composer's tone poem. Instead of the dive team that strives to rescue Ruth's body in *Saints,* he portrays a single diver, a high school biology teacher, whose encounter with the girl's body Rash details: "the blue rubbed from her eyes, flesh freed from the chandelier of bone" (49). By not assigning names to any of the story's characters, Rash makes this experience all the more universal even as he particularizes it. The springtime setting of this death, though on one hand ironic, on the other hand intimates the rebirth to which death may lead. As Rash writes of the sheriff who superintends the diver's rescue efforts, "He too had seen strange and inexplicable things involving the dead" (47). An undescribed mysterious experience the diver has beside his classroom's aquarium—the gurgle of an aquarium likewise a prominent feature of the drowning girl's final thoughts—heightens the sense of the wondrous implicit in Elizabethan usage of the term *strange*. As in several of the poems of *Among the Believers* and *Raising the Dead,* Rash leaves open the possibility of resurrection, of some alternative to death's apparent finality.

The two stories in part 3 prompted by earlier works by Rash are "The Dowry" and "Three A.M. and the Stars Were Out," both inspired by poems of the same titles, the former in *Raising the Dead,* the latter in *Waking.* The poem "The Dowry" recounts a post-Civil War sacrifice in deeply divided Madison County, where hostilities between Confederates and Lincolnites persist. When Jake Shelton asks to marry Colonel Candler's daughter Jenny, the colonel vows "no / homemade Yankee would ever / win his daughter's hand until / what he'd lost to a sniper" was restored (25). After some months pass with the colonel unappeasable, Jake brings him his own severed hand, a recurring image in Rash's work of the cost of war, that hand the dowry of the poem's title. The story expands upon and diverges from the poem in several ways: by renaming the colonel Davidson, his daughter Helen, and the Union supporter Ethan Burke; by enlarging the cast of characters to include, among others, a free-thinking physician, Noah Andrews, a disciple of Charles Darwin and T. H. Huxley; and, most important, by making a minister named William Boone its central character. It is Boone, in his seventies, who sacrifices his hand to placate Colonel Davidson, thereby preventing Ethan from amputating his own hand and jeopardizing his ability to support a wife and family.

This story not only demonstrates Rash's storytelling skills in fleshing out a situation of conflict treated briefly in a poem but also reveals the way the author formulates his artistic vision across genres and time periods through repeated use of geographical settings, family names, and subject matter. For example two different members of the Triplett family appear here, one of them having lost two brothers at Cold Harbor, a bloody Civil War battle that gives its name to one of Rash's short stories in *Casualties* and to a poem in *Waking.* The Tripletts are mentioned in several of Rash's stories, including "Last Rite" and "Return," and the Madison County setting of "The Dowry" links this story to such novels as *The World Made Straight* and *The Cove.* Thematically, too, "The Dowry" resonates deeply with other Rash texts, both in its treatment of the impact of war and in its portrait of religion and religious values. When Pastor Boone attempts to persuade Davidson to practice forgiveness and love for enemies, the colonel cites Old Testament verses advocating retribution. And when the minister points out that the colonel tends to "quote overly from the Old Testament," Davidson responds, "Yet they are cleaved together as one book. . . . Thus we choose which verses to live by" (181). Facing the colonel's intransigency, Pastor Boone considers altering his sermon text from a chapter on mercy in Acts to a verse from Obadiah: "The pride of thine own heart hath deceived thee," a crucial text in *Serena* as well (178). Even Dr. Andrews, no friend to religion, says of Davidson that he "is a man who values only his own opinion," a stance that precludes rational discussion of issues (188). This story is the third in *Nothing Gold* to allude to *The Tempest*: Dr. Andrews mentions Prospero, and Pastor Boone remarks, "Prospero forgave his enemies" (185). The extreme action the minister must take is a measure of the fallen human condition typified in the colonel's hard-heartedness. But in that action Rash also affirms human beings' capacity for selfless love and concern for others. Moreover it is the New Testament to which Rash gives the story's final words, with Pastor Boone quoting from the Gospel of Mark. Forgiveness and love, not retribution, are among the touchstones of Rash's religious views.

"Three A.M. and the Stars Were Out," the book's final story, also diverges from the dramatic monologue out of which it originated. In creating the third-person narrative of this story, elegiac in tone, Rash chose to emphasize the friendship between the veterinarian who speaks the poem and the farmer whose calf the vet helps birth. Both Carson, the veterinarian, and Darnell are veterans of the Korean War, during which they vowed that if they survived the protracted and bloody battle at Chosin Reservoir they would "stay put and grow old together" in Madison County (231). In this story Rash again employs the agrarian setting so familiar in his work, and although he does not idealize farm life, he does point out its principal benefit: its immersion of the farmer in nature, in something larger than the human community alone. The two friends, now in their seventies, succeed, on this occasion, in getting the calf born, an event about which Darnell declares, "There's a wonder to it yet" (235). For Rash that capacity for wonder is an essential dimension not only of artistic creation and religious consciousness but also of distinctively human identity. The story's—and the book's—closing image is that of Darnell standing in the doorway of his barn, "attentive as any good sentry," a simile that posits the presence, or potential presence, of danger and therefore the need for vigilance. But the French etymology of the word *sentry,* derived from *sentinel* and its French and Latin roots *sentir/sentīre,* links a sentry not just to keenness of perception but to depth of feeling. Such attentiveness to the natural world and to other people is precisely what Rash's fiction and poetry cultivate. Both Carson and Darnell express satisfaction with the shape their lives have assumed, and the book thus ends with a story of birth, not death; of calm, not violence; of friendship, not animosity.

The two stories that precede "Three A.M." are likewise tales of success, not defeat. "The Woman at the Pond," a first-person narrative set in Cleveland County, where the stories of *The Night the New Jesus Fell to Earth* take place, interweaves the narrator's recollection of a past event at a farm pond with the pond's being drained in the present. In striking contrast to the many images of flooding in Rash's work, of whole valleys being inundated, this is a story of exposure, not erasure. The narrator's fear that the woman he encountered at the pond as a seventeen-year-old was murdered there, her body concealed under the water, proves unjustified. While the ultimate fate of this woman remains uncertain, the narrator realizes that his failure to contact the police did not result in her death. The past clearly impinges on the present in this story, as in much of Rash's writing, but the draining of the pond unburdens the narrator. Rather than focusing on negative character traits, as Jollimore contends in his review cited earlier, Rash here presents a figure of conscience and concern for others, like Pastor Boone of "The Dowry."

"Night Hawks" (the story's title echoes that of Edward Hopper's iconic painting *Nighthawks*) depicts a more complicated character, Ginny Atwell, who is scarred both literally and figuratively by a past event, an injury to a child in her sixth-grade classroom that led her to disfigure her own face with a shard of glass from the same storm-broken window that struck her student. As the story begins, Ginny, having quit teaching, becomes a late-night disc jockey, her radio moniker the Night Hawk. The opening sentence refers to Ginny's conviction, at her interview for this job, that "she could not have picked a better place to begin again" (209). Three months later she seems to have been proven correct, for as she signs off the air, she plays the Eagles' "Already Gone," an upbeat tune whose lyrics insist, "I'm feelin' strong / I will sing this vict'ry song." Ginny's suffering, like that the conductor Goritz commends to Walter in *The Cove*, enables her to reach out to others. Yet Rash also portrays Ginny as choosing isolation, as needlessly rejecting the love offered by Andrew, the art teacher who had shown Hopper's painting to her class.

In addressing the themes of suffering, isolation, and interpersonal communication, "Night Hawks" becomes something of an *ars poetica* for Rash. The plural noun of the story's title suggests that others share Ginny's wounded condition and her sense of isolation. In her role as DJ, however, quizzing her listeners on a Frost poem, Ginny becomes an artist figure, managing to transcend her separate selfhood and touch others. The Frost text whose opening line Ginny quotes is "Stopping by Woods on a Snowy Evening," a poem that images an isolated human figure but that also conveys the speaker's sense of having an active future, one filled with "promises to keep, / And miles to go before I sleep."[21] The story's closing paragraphs likewise present Ginny anticipating the future, not trapped in the past, envisioning her evening's work: "Ginny would speak to people in bedrooms, to clerks drenched in the fluorescent light of convenience stores, to millworkers driving back roads home after graveyard shifts. She would speak to the drunk and sober, the godly and the godless. All the while high above where she sat, the station's red beacon would pulse like a heart, as if giving bearings to all those in the dark adrift and alone" (225).

The inclusiveness of Ginny's projected audience, her embrace of contrasting types of people, reflects Rash's desire to address universal concerns, to encompass both the particularities and the commonalities of human experience. The simile involving the beacon pulsing "like a heart" again invokes the creation of empathy as one of the most important functions of the literary arts, which for Rash clearly have a didactic role to play in "giving bearings" to the reader, in nurturing the reader's capacity to make judgments, including moral judgments. A hawk's keenness of vision ties this story to the book's concluding image of Darnell as sentry. Although Rash inserts the qualifying phrase "as if" in the story's final sentence ("as if giving bearings"), his enduring interest in Frost's work and his allusions to Frost both in this story and in the book's title might lead readers familiar with Frost's prose to recall the motto with which he closes his essay on Edwin Arlington Robinson: "All virtue in 'as if.'"[22] As a title, of course, *Nothing Gold Can Stay* is far less optimistic than *Raising the Dead* or *The World Made Straight,* but the stories in this collection are scarcely the "cycle of pessimism" that Cook claims. Along with their accounts of treachery, folly, and the wreckage caused by drug addiction, they also offer memorable instances of friendship, self-sacrifice, love, and compassion.

For nearly three decades Rash's literary reputation has steadily grown, having now achieved international stature. Yet he often remains relegated to "regional" status here in the United States. As recently as 2013, even so strong a supporter of his work as Janet Maslin referred to Rash as an Appalachian author.[23] While for Maslin that term was meant to be descriptive, not reductive, for many readers, reviewers, and literary critics, such labels justify a dismissive attitude toward writers they consider "only" or "just" regional. As this study has tried to indicate, Rash grounds himself in the landscape of his ancestors, particularly the mountains of western North Carolina, but he does so to address such universal concerns as war, death, human beings' relationship to nature, family ties, and the impact of social and economic upheavals on people's lives. What Rash has the narrator of "Waiting for the End of the World" say of Lynyrd Skynyrd might be said to apply to the author's own work: "Skynyrd never pruned their Southern musical roots to give them 'national appeal,' and that gave their music, whatever else its failings, an honesty and an edge" (*Burning Bright* 189). Rash's fiction and poetry have that honesty and edge and merit the quality of attention they will surely receive from general readers and critics alike in the years ahead.

NOTES

Chapter 1—Understanding Ron Rash

    1. Rash, "Importance of Place."

    2. Mudge, "Shaped by the Land."

    3. Anderson, "Twisting," 116.

    4. Wickett, "Ron Rash."

    5. Bain and Flora, *Contemporary Poets,* 14.

    6. Marion, "Ron Rash," 18.

    7. Brown, "Blood-Memory," 342.

    8. Ibid.

    9. Rash, "Gift of Silence."

    10. Rash, "Importance of Place."

    11. Hoffman and Shurbutt, "Ron Rash," 63.

    12. Brown, "Blood-Memory," 339.

    13. Charlotte Mecklenburg Library, "Meet the Author."

    14. Metcalfe, "Small Talk."

    15. Birnbaum, "Ron Rash."

    16. Brown, "Blood-Memory," 339.

    17. Hoffman and Shurbutt, "Ron Rash," 60.

    18. Marion, "Ron Rash," 23.

    19. Wilhelm and Graves, "Interview," 236.

    20. Brown, "Blood-Memory," 340.

    21. Wilhelm and Graves, "Interview," 217.

    22. Eller, *Uneven Ground,* 29, 30.

    23. Marion, "Ron Rash," 20, 21.

    24. Shuler, "Ron Rash," 12.

    25. Hauck and Basl, "Ron Rash."

    26. Bjerre, "Natural World," 226–27.

Chapter 2—*The Night the New Jesus Fell to Earth, Casualties,* and *Chemistry*

    1. North Carolina Arts Council, "Ron Rash."

    2. Hauck and Basl, "Ron Rash."

    3. Bjerre, "Natural World," 223.

    4. Rash, *New Jesus,* 37, 43. All further quotations from this book are cited parenthetically.

    5. Wilhelm and Graves, "Interview," 224.

    6. Lee, "Upstate Writers."

7. Birnbaum, "Rash, Redux."
8. Brown, "Blood-Memory," 349.
9. Wickett, "Ron Rash."
10. Allen, review of *New Jesus*, 754.
11. Mincey, "Ron Rash."
12. Anderson, "Twisting," 112.
13. Hoffman and Shurbutt, "Ron Rash," 60.
14. Snodgrass, "Crass Casualty," 645; Keene, "News," 146.
15. Greene, review of *Casualties*, 365.
16. Rash, *Casualties*, 16, 17 [26, 27]. All further quotations from this book are cited parenthetically, with the bracketed page numbers those of the stories reprinted in Rash's *Chemistry and Other Stories*. Where a quoted passage was revised for publication in *Chemistry and Other Stories*, the abbreviation "cf." precedes the bracketed page number.
17. Pascal, *Pensées*, 95.
18. Bjerre, "Natural World," 225.
19. Higgins, "Anything," 52.
20. *Kill Your Darlings*, "Conversation," 131.
21. Bjerre, "Natural World," 222–23.
22. Makuck, review of *Chemistry*.
23. Smith, *Stevie Smith*, 128.
24. Frost, *Complete Poems*, 328.
25. Mincey, "Ron Rash."
26. Antopol, review of *Chemistry*, 202, 203.
27. Fisher, review of *Chemistry*, 85; Wilhelm, review of *Chemistry*, 111.
28. Wilhelm, review of *Chemistry*, 111.
29. Yeats, *Collected Poems*, 292–93.
30. Rash, *Chemistry*, 2. All further quotations from this book are cited parenthetically.
31. Emerson, *Essays*, 41.

Chapter 3—*Eureka Mill, Among the Believers, Raising the Dead,* and *Waking*

1. Hecht, "Gift," xi.
2. Shuler, "Ron Rash," 15.
3. Brown, "Blood-Memory," 348.
4. Marion, "Ron Rash," 31.
5. Wilhelm, "Ghostly Bodies," 26; Brown, "Dark and Clear Vision," 19.
6. Blake, *Poetry and Prose*, 95.
7. Rash, *Eureka Mill*, xiii; Tannenbaum, *Darker Phases*, 46. All further quotations from *Eureka Mill* are cited parenthetically.
8. Brown, "Blood-Memory," 352; Bjerre, "Natural World," 226.
9. West, "Of Looms and Fatelooms," 76; Jolliff, review of *Eureka Mill*, 64, 66.
10. Eller, *Miners, Millhands*, 126.
11. Rash, *Among the Believers*, ix. All further quotations from this book are cited parenthetically.
12. Quoted by House, "Making," 14.
13. Hoffman and Shurbutt, "Ron Rash," 61.
14. Quoted by Smith, "Words," 17.

15. Marion, "Ron Rash," 36.
16. Rash, "Shelton Laurel," 114; Rash, "Facts of Historical Fiction," 78.
17. Bjerre, "Natural World," 225.
18. The table of contents in *Among the Believers* lists this poem's title correctly, but due to a typesetting error, on p. 59 the date precedes "Morning Service."
19. Asfoxseesit, "Ron Rash."
20. Brown, "Blood-Memory," 341.
21. Vaughan, *Complete Poetry*, 271.
22. Chappell, review of *Among the Believers*, 228.
23. Ibid.
24. Bjerre, "Natural World," 222–23.
25. Rash, classroom remarks at Emory & Henry College, October 24, 2003.
26. Rash, *Raising the Dead*, xi. All further quotations from this book are cited parenthetically.
27. Campion, "Forms of Reckoning," 94.
28. McInerney, "Glimmering Substance," 82.
29. Frost, *Complete Poems*, 520–21.
30. Brown, "Blood-Memory," 348. Rash also paraphrases "Resolution" in his interview with Marion ("Ron Rash," 40), an interview conducted in 1999, more than a decade before the poem was collected in *Waking*.
31. Rash, *Waking*, xi. All further quotations from this book are cited parenthetically.
32. Brown, "Blood-Memory," 341.
33. Hoffman and Shurbutt, "Ron Rash," 62.
34. Wordsworth, *Selected Poems*, 345.
35. Bizzaro, "Poets' Demands," 39.
36. Rash et al., "Nature, Place," 21.
37. West, review of *Waking*, 304.
38. Dickinson, *Complete Poems*, 576–77.
39. Hoffman and Shurbutt, "Ron Rash," 62.

Chapter 4—*One Foot in Eden, Saints at the River,* and *The World Made Straight*

1. Birnbaum, "Ron Rash"; Rozzo, "First Fiction."
2. *Kill Your Darlings*, "Conversation," 119.
3. Anderson, "Twisting," 110–11.
4. *Kill Your Darlings*, "Conversation," 120.
5. Hoffman and Shurbutt, "Ron Rash," 63.
6. Bjerre, "Natural World," 227.
7. Rash et al., "Continuity and Change," 54.
8. Rash, *One Foot in Eden*, ix. All further quotations from this book are cited parenthetically.
9. Muir, *Collected Poems*, 227.
10. Birnbaum, "Ron Rash."
11. *Kill Your Darlings*, "Conversation," 115.
12. Shakespeare, *First Part of King Henry IV*, III.i.50, 53.
13. See, for example, McCrumb's *The Hangman's Beautiful Daughter* (New York: Scribner, 1992).
14. Miller, "Long Remember," 206.

15. *Kill Your Darlings,* "Conversation," 125.

16. House, "Making," 13.

17. Biggers, "Out of Appalachia," 15.

18. *Kill Your Darlings,* "Conversation," 126.

19. Kingsbury, "Language."

20. Lefler, "Inside the Prism," 72.

21. Bjerre, "Natural World," 225. For a detailed discussion of the parallels and contrasts between events in the novel and the drowning on the Chattooga, see Lane, "Girl in the River," 162–67.

22. Rash, *Saints at the River,* 56. All further quotations from this book are cited parenthetically.

23. Asfoxseesit, "Ron Rash."

24. James, *Varieties of Religious Experience,* 372. A typo in the novel's epigraph substitutes *rights* for *lights.* Further quotations from James's book are cited parenthetically.

25. Shurbutt, "Burning Bright," 37.

26. Anderson, "Twisting," 114.

27. Woodside, review of *Saints at the River,* 235.

28. Lefler, "Inside the Prism," 76.

29. Birnbaum, "Ron Rash."

30. Holt published the paperback edition of *One Foot in Eden* but not the hardbound.

31. Rash, *World Made Straight,* 159 (Rash's italics). All further quotations from this book are cited parenthetically.

32. Harington, "N.C. History"; Lopez, review of *World Made Straight,* 248, 249.

33. Rash, "Shelton Laurel," 114.

34. Bjerre, "Natural World," 220.

35. Rash, "Facts of Historical Fiction," 78; Bjerre, "Natural World," 220.

36. Paludan, *Victims,* ix, xx.

37. Rash, "Facts of Historical Fiction," 78.

38. Rash, "Shelton Laurel," 116, 114.

39. Drawing on an article in the *New York Times* of July 24, 1863, Rash gives David Shelton's age as twelve, while Paludan says he was thirteen. According to Paludan, the date of the massacre is likewise uncertain. Whereas he suggests January 18 is "highly likely" (139), he concedes that a later date is possible. In "Shelton Laurel" Rash states that the massacre occurred on January 23 (115), but in *The World Made Straight* he appears to use January 18 (204).

40. Paludan, *Victims,* 21–22.

41. Rash's uncle makes a similar comment to young Ron in "Shelton Laurel," 114.

42. Weil, "*Iliad,*" 171, 184–85.

43. Ibid., 192.

44. Rash, "Facts of Historical Fiction," 78.

45. Lopez, review of *World Made Straight,* 248.

46. Hauck and Basl, "Ron Rash."

47. Brown, "Blood-Memory," 349.

Chapter 5—*Serena* and *The Cove*

1. Maslin, "Couple Creates an Empire."

2. Parini, review of *Serena*.

3. Birnbaum, "Rash, Redux."

4. Mincey, "Interview."

5. Quoted by Brown, "Rash's *Serena*," 76.

6. Marlowe, *Complete Plays*, 301, scene ii, lines 97–98.

7. Brown, "Rash's *Serena*," 76.

8. Ibid.; Levin, *Overreacher*.

9. Brown, "Rash's *Serena*," 76.

10. Quoted by Brown, "Rash's *Serena*," 78.

11. Rash, *Serena*, 3. All further quotations from this novel are cited parenthetically.

12. O'Connor, "Author's Note," 5.

13. Fitzgerald, *Gatsby*, 180–81. Rash also uses songs that appear in Fitzgerald's novel (96–97) in chapter 24 of *Serena*.

14. Shurbutt, "Burning Bright," 48.

15. On September 22, 2006, during a panel discussion at Emory & Henry College, Rash said of McCarthy's *The Road*, "It's a great book, an important book, one that in its dealing with the natural world is as important as any other I can think of" (Rash et al., "Nature, Place," 22).

16. Rash quotes from the King James Version of the Bible, but the other quotations from Obadiah are taken from the Revised Standard Version.

17. Asfoxseesit, Ron Rash.

18. Maslin, "Out of Sight"; Charles, "Rash's *The Cove*."

19. In addition to the reviews by Maslin and Charles, see Le Guin, review of *The Cove*.

20. Painter, *German Invasion*, 5; Braynard, "*World's Greatest Ship*," 118.

21. Rash, *Cove*, 1. All further quotations from this novel are cited parenthetically.

22. Martin, "Ron Rash's 'The Cove.'"

23. Julius Caesar, *The Gallic War* (Cambridge, Mass.: Harvard University Press, 1979), 162.

24. Because U.S. conscripts like Hank did not reach France until May 1918, the novel's chronicling of events is somewhat askew, for readers are told that Hank was still overseas in the fall of 1917.

25. Painter, *German Invasion*, 36. According to Painter, that prisoner was not one of those interned from the *Vaterland*.

26. Whitman, *Leaves of Grass*, 88.

27. Byron, *Selected Poetry*, 294.

28. Maslin, "Out of Sight."

29. Mudge, "Shaped by the Land."

Chapter 6 — *Burning Bright* and *Nothing Gold Can Stay*

1. Maslin, "Be Careful."

2. Blake, *Poetry and Prose*, 24–25.

3. Rash, *Raising the Dead*, 51; see the similar episode in chapter 7 of *Serena* in which the thief turns out to be a raccoon that Rachel Harmon catches and kills.

4. Rash, *Burning Bright*, 6. All further quotations from this book are cited parenthetically.

5. Paludan, *Victims*, 96.

6. Twain, *Huckleberry Finn*, 37, 84.

7. Rash's revision of "Return" omits the protagonist's name, has another soldier refer to him as a "hillbilly," and makes many other changes in diction and phrasing.

8. Yeats, *Collected Poems*, 184–85.

9. Conrad, *Heart of Darkness*, 66.

10. Rash, "Shelton Laurel," 114.

11. Reid, review of *Nothing Gold Can Stay*.

12. Cook, "*Nothing Gold*."

13. Jollimore, review of *Nothing Gold Can Stay*.

14. Frost, *Complete Poems*, 272.

15. Rash, *Nothing Gold Can Stay*, 5. All further quotations from this book are cited parenthetically.

16. Because the U.S. draft lottery to which Rash refers in this story went into effect in December 1969, the July setting of "The Magic Bus" means that the story's action occurs no earlier than the summer of 1970.

17. Weller, *Yesterday's People*.

18. The ballad about Glencoe that Rash quotes is not a traditional ballad but was composed by Jim McLean in the 1960s (http://www.contemplator.com/scotland/glen _coe.html, accessed May 13, 2013).

19. Noel S. McFerran, "The Massacre at Glencoe," http://www.jacobite.ca/songs/ massacre.htm (accessed May 13, 2013).

20. Shakespeare, *Tempest*, I.ii.399–404.

21. Frost, *Complete Poems*, 275.

22. Frost, *Selected Prose*, 67.

23. Maslin, "Be Careful."

BIBLIOGRAPHY

Primary Works

BOOKS BY RASH

Among the Believers. Oak Ridge, Tenn.: Iris, 2000.
Burning Bright. New York: HarperCollins, 2010.
Casualties. Beaufort, S.C.: Bench Press, 2000.
Chemistry and Other Stories. New York: Picador, 2007.
The Cove. New York: HarperCollins, 2012.
Eureka Mill. Corvallis, Ore.: Bench Press, 1998.
The Night the New Jesus Fell to Earth and Other Stories from Cliffside, North Carolina. Columbia, S.C.: Bench Press, 1994.
Nothing Gold Can Stay. New York: HarperCollins, 2013.
One Foot in Eden. Charlotte, N.C.: Novello Festival Press, 2002.
Raising the Dead. Oak Ridge, Tenn.: Iris, 2002.
Saints at the River. New York: Holt, 2004.
Serena. New York: HarperCollins, 2008.
Waking. Spartanburg, S.C.: Hub City, 2011.
The World Made Straight. New York: Holt, 2006.

ESSAYS BY RASH

"The Facts of Historical Fiction." *Publishers Weekly,* April 10, 2006, 78.
"The Gift of Silence." HarperCollins Publishers. http://www.harpercollins.com/author/microsite/readingguide.aspx?authorID=33503&displayType=essay&articleId=6058 (accessed December 13, 2012).
"The Importance of Place." Rusoff Agency and Associates. http://www.rusoffagency.com/authors/rash_r/ron_rash_onwriting.htm (accessed December 5, 2012).
"In the Beginning." *Wall Street Journal,* March 9, 2013.
"Ron Rash." In *Southern Appalachian Poetry: An Anthology of Works by 37 Poets,* edited by Marita Garin, 177–78. Jefferson, N.C.: McFarland, 2008.
"Serena." http://www.powells.com/essays/ronrash.html (accessed November 27, 2012).
"Shelton Laurel." *North Carolina Literary Review* 17 (2008): 114–16.

PANEL DISCUSSIONS

"Continuity and Change: Future Directions in Appalachian Literature." *Iron Mountain Review* 23 (2007): 53–57.

"Nature, Place, and the Appalachian Writer." *Iron Mountain Review* 23 (2007): 18–24.

Secondary Sources

ARTICLES

Baldwin, Kara. "'Incredible Eloquence': How Ron Rash's Novels Keep the Celtic Literary Tradition Alive." *South Carolina Review* 39, no. 1 (2006): 37–46.

Bjerre, Thomas Ærvold. "Ron Rash: *One Foot in Eden.*" In *Still in Print: The Southern Novel Today,* edited by Jan Nordby Gretlund, 233–47. Columbia: University of South Carolina Press, 2010.

Boyleston, Matthew. "Wild Boar in These Woods: The Influence of Seamus Heaney on the Poetry of Ron Rash." *South Carolina Review* 41, no. 2 (2009): 11–17.

Brown, Joyce Compton. "The Dark and Clear Vision of Ron Rash." *Appalachian Heritage* 30, no. 4 (2002): 15–24.

Brown, Joyce Compton, and Mark Powell. "Ron Rash's *Serena* and the 'Blank and Pitiless Gaze' of Exploitation in Appalachia." *North Carolina Literary Review* 19 (2010): 70–89.

Graves, Jesse. "Lattice Work: Formal Tendencies in the Poetry of Robert Morgan and Ron Rash." *Southern Quarterly* 45, no. 1 (2007): 78–86.

Hecht, Anthony. "A Gift Matched with Skills of the First Order." In *Among the Believers,* xi–xv. Oak Ridge, Tenn.: Iris, 2000.

Higgins, Anna Dunlap. "'Anything but Surrender': Preserving Southern Appalachia in the Works of Ron Rash." *North Carolina Literary Review* 13 (2004): 49–58.

House, Silas. "Making Himself Heard." *Appalachian Heritage* 30, no. 4 (2002): 11–14.

———. "A Matter of Life and Death: Old and New Appalachia Meet in *One Foot in Eden.*" *Iron Mountain Review* 20 (2004): 21–25.

Hovis, George. "The Legacy of Thomas Wolfe in Contemporary Appalachian Fiction: Four Recent North Carolina Novels." *Thomas Wolfe Review* 36 (2012): 70–91.

Lane, John. "The Girl in the River: The Wild and Scenic Chattooga, Ron Rash's *Saints at the River,* and the Drowning of Rachel Trois." *South Carolina Review* 41, no. 1 (2008): 162–67.

Lee, Anna. "Upstate Writers Ron Rash and George Singleton Share 20 Years of Storytelling." http://www.greenvilleonline.com/article/20121120/LIFE/311200030/Upstate-writers-Ron-Rash-and-George-Singleton-share-20-years-of-storytelling (accessed November 27, 2012).

Lefler, Susan M. "Inside the Prism: Themes That Flow throughout Ron Rash's Works." *Appalachian Heritage* 32, no. 4 (2004): 72–77.

Miller, Mindy Beth. "Long Remember, Long Recall: The Preservation of Appalachian Regional Heritage in Ron Rash's *One Foot in Eden.*" *Journal of Kentucky Studies* 26 (2009): 198–209.

Peeler, Tim. "Resting on the Gift of Their Labors: The Poetry of Ron Rash." *Iron Mountain Review* 20 (2004): 7–12.

Shurbutt, Sylvia Bailey. "'Burning Bright': Language, Place, and Storytelling in the Poetry and Prose of Ron Rash." *Anthology of Appalachian Writers* 4 (2012): 18–56.

Smith, Jimmy Dean. "Spirit Country: The Voice of the Earth and Ron Rash's Southern Appalachia." *North Carolina Literary Review* 20 (2011): 111–20.

Smith, Newton. "Words to Raise the Dead: The Poetry of Ron Rash." *Iron Mountain Review* 20 (2004): 13–20.

Vernon, Zachary. "The Role of Witness: Ron Rash's Peculiarly Historical Consciousness." *South Carolina Review* 42, no. 2 (2010): 19–24.

Wilhelm, Randall. "Ghostly Bodies and Worker Voices: Power and Resistance in Ron Rash's *Eureka Mill*." *South Carolina Review* 42, no. 2 (2010): 25–36.

INTERVIEWS

Anderson, Forrest. "Twisting the Radio Dial: An Interview with Ron Rash." *Southeast Review* 25, no. 2 (2007): 104–17.

Asfoxseesit. "My January [2010] Interview with Ron Rash." September 10, 2010. http://foxofbama.blogspot.com/2010/09/my-january-interview-with-ron-rash.html.

Biggers, Jeff. "Out of Appalachia: New Writing from an Old Region, Including an Interview with Gretchen Laskas and Ron Rash." *Bloomsbury Review,* July–August 2003, 14–15.

Birnbaum, Robert. "Ron Rash." *Morning News,* November 7, 2005. http://www .themorningnews.org/article/ron-rash (accessed November 27, 2012).

———. "Ron Rash, Redux." *Morning News,* August 29, 2012. http://www.the morningnews.org/article/ron-rash-redux (accessed December 13, 2012).

Bjerre, Thomas Ærvold. "'The Natural World Is the Most Universal of Languages': An Interview with Ron Rash." *Appalachian Journal* 34 (2007): 216–27.

Brown, Joyce Compton. "The Power of Blood-Memory." In *Appalachia and Beyond: Conversations with Writers from the Mountain South,* edited by John Lang, 337–53. Knoxville: University of Tennessee Press, 2006.

Charlotte Mecklenburg Library. "Meet the Author: Ron Rash." http://www .cmlibrary.org/readers_club/meetAuthor.asp?author=53 (accessed November 27, 2012).

Charney, Noah. "Ron Rash: How I Write." *Daily Beast,* February 27, 2013. http:// www.thedailybeast.com/articles/2013/02/27/ron-rash-how-i-write.html.

Hauck, Jeremy, and Kevin Basl. "An Interview with Ron Rash." *Tinge Magazine.* http://www.tingemagazine.org/an-interview-with-ron-rash/ (accessed November 27, 2012).

Hoffman, David O., and Sylvia Bailey Shurbutt. "Interview with Ron Rash." *Anthology of Appalachian Writers* 4 (2012): 60–63.

"*Kill Your Darlings* in Conversation with Ron Rash." *Kill Your Darlings* 6 (July 2011): 111–32.

Kingsbury, Pam. "Language Can Be Magical: An Interview with Ron Rash." *Southern Scribe.* http://www.southernscribe.com/zine/authors/Rash_Ron.htm (accessed May 10, 2012).

Marion, Jeff Daniel. "Interview with Ron Rash." *Mossy Creek Reader* 9 (2000): 18–40.

Metcalfe, Anna. "Small Talk: Ron Rash." *Financial Times,* March 9, 2012. http:// www.ft.com/cms/s/2/d6eeoa8c-687b-11e1-a6cc-00144feabdco.html.

Mincey, Marann. "An Interview with Ron Rash." *Pedestal Magazine.* http://www .pedestalmagazine.com/gallery.php?item=2949 (accessed October 28, 2013)

Mudge, Alden. "Shaped by the Land, Torn Apart by Intolerance: Interview." *Book Page,* April 2012. http://bookpage.com/interview/shaped-by-the-land-torn-apart -by-intolerance.

North Carolina Arts Council. "Ron Rash." North Carolina Literary Trails. http://
www.ncliterarytrails.org/featuredwriters/ronrash.aspx (accessed December 13,
2012).

Shuler, Jack. "An Interview with Ron Rash." *South Carolina Review* 33, no. 1 (2000):
11–16.

Wickett, Dan. "An Interview with Ron Rash." Emerging Writers Network, April
8, 2012. http://emergingwriters.typepad.com/emerging_writers_network/2012/04/
celebration-of-the-release-of-The-Cove-by-Ron-Rash.html.

Wilhelm, Randall, and Jesse Graves. "Interview: Words with Ron Rash." *Grist* 1
(2008): 214–40.

Zacharias, Karen Spears. "Ron Rash." Authors 'round the South, September
21, 2006. http://www.authorsroundthesouth.com/author-2-author/139-ron-rash
-speaks-with-karen-spears-zacharias.

SELECTED REVIEWS

The Night the New Jesus Fell to Earth

Allen, Gilbert. Untitled review. *Georgia Review* 49 (1995): 753–54.

Eureka Mill

Jolliff, William. Untitled review. *Appalachian Heritage* 27, no. 3 (1999): 64–66.

Lang, John. Untitled review. *Appalachian Journal* 26 (1998): 61–66.

West, Robert. "Of Looms and Fatelooms." *Carolina Quarterly* 50, no. 3 (1998):
74–76.

Among the Believers

Chappell, Fred. Untitled review. *Appalachian Journal* 28 (2001): 228–31.

Core, George. Untitled review. *Sewanee Review* 109 (2001): iv–v.

West, Robert. "In Another Country." *Asheville Poetry Review* 8 (2001): 25–29.

Worthington, Marianne. Untitled review. *Appalachian Heritage* 28, no. 4 (2000):
61–64.

Casualties

Greene, Jonathan. Untitled review. *Appalachian Journal* 28 (2001): 363–65.

Keene, Jarret. "The News from Rash's South." *Chattahoochee Review* 21 (2000):
145–46.

Snodgrass, Kathleen. "Crass Casualty." *Georgia Review* 55 (2001): 645–47.

Raising the Dead

Campion, Peter. "Forms of Reckoning." *Poetry,* May 2003, 93–94.

Dings, Fred. "Drowned Voices." *Quarterly West* 54 (2002): 124–26.

Hummell, Austin. Untitled review. *Passages North* 23 (2002): 179–84.

McInerney, Stephen. "Glimmering Substance." *Quadrant,* March 2003, 82–84.

One Foot in Eden

Dunn, Tim. Untitled review. *Journal of Appalachian Studies* 10.1–2 (2004): 206–7.

McVoy, Terra Elan. "Repopulating the Southern Landscape." *Chattahoochee Review*
25, no. 3 (2005): 125–28.

Rozzo, Mark. "First Fiction." *Los Angeles Times,* December 29, 2002.

Saints at the River

McVoy, Terra Elan. "Repopulating the Southern Landscape." *Chattahoochee Review* 25, no. 3 (2005): 125–28.

Woodside, Jane Harris. Untitled review. *Appalachian Journal* 33 (2006): 233–35.

The World Made Straight

Biggers, Jeff. Untitled review. *Appalachian Journal* 34 (2007): 245–47.

Harington, Donald. "N.C. History Haunts Fine New Novel." *Raleigh News and Observer,* April 30, 2006. http://www.newsobserver.com/2006/04/30/94401/nc -history-haunts-fine-new-novel.html.

Lopez, Lorraine M. Untitled review. *Southern Review* 43 (2007): 247–49.

Wilhelm, Randall. Untitled review. *Appalachian Heritage* 34, no. 4 (2006): 94–96.

Chemistry and Other Stories

Antopol, Molly. Untitled review. *Southern Review* 44 (2008): 202–4.

Fisher, Ann H. Untitled review. *Library Journal,* April 1, 2007, 85.

Makuck, Peter. "Rash Turns to Fish Tales." *Raleigh News and Observer,* July 8, 2007.

Wilhelm, Randall. Untitled review. *Appalachian Heritage* 35, no. 4 (2007): 110–12.

Serena

Brown, Joyce Compton. Untitled review. *Appalachian Heritage* 37, no. 1 (2009): 61–64.

Charles, Ron. "The Murderess of Smoky Mountain." *Washington Post,* October 12, 2008.

Loving, Denton. Untitled review. *Appalachian Journal* 36 (2008–9): 105–8.

Maslin, Janet. "Couple Creates an Empire by Felling Trees and Anyone in Their Way." *New York Times,* October 6, 2008.

Parini, Jay. Untitled review. *Guardian,* October 9, 2009. http://www.guardian.com/ books/2009/oct/10/serena-ron-rash-review.

Powell, Mark. Untitled review. *Southern Quarterly* 47, no. 3 (2010): 202–4.

Burning Bright

Johnstone, Doug. Untitled review. *Independent,* August 21, 2011. http://www.inde pendent.co.uk/arts-entertainment/books/reviews/burning-bright-by-ron-rash.

Maslin, Janet. "Rural Pride and Poverty and a Hen's Empty Nest." *New York Times,* March 8, 2010.

Rouse, Viki Dasher. Untitled review. *Appalachian Heritage* 39, no. 3 (2011): 102–3.

Waking

Belcher, Philip. Untitled review. *Shenandoah* 61, no. 2 (2012). http://shenandoahliter ary.org/612/waking-by-ron-rash.

Bizzaro, Patrick. "Poets' Demands: Readers and Contexts in Four New Books of Poetry." *Asheville Poetry Review* 18, no. 1 (2011): 32–51.

Vernon, Zachary. "The Poet's Native Tongue." *Carolina Quarterly* 62, no. 1 (2012): 112–15.

West, Robert. Untitled review. *Journal of Appalachian Studies* 18.1–2 (2012): 302–5.

The Cove

Charles, Ron. "Ron Rash's *The Cove* Doesn't Have the Energy of His Masterpiece, *Serena*." *Washington Post,* April 3, 2012.

Le Guin, Ursula K. Untitled review. *Guardian,* March 16, 2012. http://www.guardian .co.uk/books/2012/mar/16/the-cove-ron-rash-review.

Martin, D. G. "Ron Rash's 'The Cove'—Laurel Shelton or Shelton Laurel." Chapel boro.com, April 8, 2012. http://chapelboro.com/pages/10065369php?archive=1&p id=231614.

Maslin, Janet. "Out of Sight in Wartime." *New York Times,* April 2, 2012.

Nothing Gold Can Stay

Cook, Liz. "*Nothing Gold Can Stay* Compiles Stories of Bleak Luck." *Kansas City Star,* February 21, 2013. http://www.kansascity.com/2013/02/21/4078714/book-review -nothing-gold-can-stay.html.

Jollimore, Troy. Untitled review. *Chicago Tribune,* February 15, 2013. http://articles.chi cagotribune.com/2013–02–15/features/ct-prj-0217-nothing-gold-can-stay-ron-rash.

Maslin, Janet. "Be Careful of the Locals: They're Tough." *New York Times,* February 28, 2013.

Reid, Graham. Untitled review. *New Zealand Herald,* March 16, 2013. http://www .nzherald.co.nz/lifestyle/news/article.cfm?c_id=6&objectid=10871037.

Webb, Gina. "Rash Offers Hard Truths, Tender Mercies in Stories." *Atlanta Journal-Constitution,* March 10, 2013.

OTHER WORKS CITED

Bain, Robert, and Joseph M. Flora, eds. *Contemporary Poets, Dramatists, Essayists, and Novelists of the South: A Bio-bibliographic Sourcebook.* Westport, Conn.: Greenwood, 1994.

Blake, William. *The Poetry and Prose of William Blake.* Edited by David V. Erdman. Garden City, N.Y.: Doubleday, 1970.

Braynard, Frank O. "*World's Greatest Ship*": *The Story of the LEVIATHAN,* vol. 1. New York: South Street Seaport Museum, 1972.

Conrad, Joseph. *Heart of Darkness.* Edited by Ross C. Murfin. New York: St. Martin's, 1989.

Dickinson, Emily. *The Complete Poems of Emily Dickinson.* Edited by Thomas H. Johnson. Boston: Little, Brown, 1960.

Eller, Ronald D. *Uneven Ground: Appalachia since 1945.* Lexington: University Press of Kentucky, 2008.

———. *Miners, Millhands, and Mountaineers: Industrialization of the Appalachian South, 1880–1930.* Knoxville: University of Tennessee Press, 1982.

Emerson, Ralph Waldo. *Essays and Lectures.* New York: Library of America, 1983.

Fitzgerald, F. Scott. *The Great Gatsby.* New York: Scribner, 1966.

Frost, Robert. *Complete Poems of Robert Frost.* New York: Holt, Rinehart and Winston, 1949.

Gordon, George, Lord Byron. *The Selected Poetry of Lord Byron.* Edited by Leslie A. Marchand. New York: Modern Library, 1951.

James, William. *The Varieties of Religious Experience: A Study in Human Nature.* New York: Modern Library, 1994.

Levin, Harry. *The Overreacher: A Study of Christopher Marlowe.* Cambridge, Mass.: Harvard University Press, 1952.

Marlowe, Christopher. *The Complete Plays.* Edited by Mark Thornton Burnett. London: Dent, 1999.

Muir, Edwin. *Collected Poems.* New York: Oxford University Press, 1965.

O'Connor, Flannery. "Author's Note to the Second Edition." In *Wise Blood.* New York: Farrar, Straus & Cudahy, 1962.

Painter, Jacqueline Burgin. *The German Invasion of Western North Carolina: A Pictorial History.* Johnson City, Tenn.: Overmountain, 1992.

Paludan, Phillip Shaw. *Victims: A True Story of the Civil War.* Knoxville: University of Tennessee Press, 2004.

Pascal, Blaise. *Pensées.* Translated by W. F. Trotter. New York: Modern Library, 1941.

Shakespeare, William. *The First Part of King Henry IV.* Edited by A. R. Humphreys. London: Methuen, 1967.

———. *The Tempest.* Edited by Frank Kermode. London: Methuen, 1972.

Smith, Stevie. *Stevie Smith: A Selection.* Edited by Hermione Lee. London: Faber & Faber, 1983.

Tannenbaum, Frank. *Darker Phases of the South.* New York: Putnam, 1924.

Twain, Mark. *Adventures of Huckleberry Finn.* Edited by Sculley Bradley et al. New York: Norton, 1962.

Vaughan, Henry. *The Complete Poetry of Henry Vaughan.* Edited by French Fogle. New York: New York University Press, 1965.

Weil, Simone. *Simone Weil: An Anthology.* Edited by Siân Miles. New York: Weidenfeld & Nicolson, 1986.

Weller, Jack E. *Yesterday's People: Life in Contemporary Appalachia.* Lexington: University of Kentucky Press, 1965.

Whitman, Walt. *Leaves of Grass.* Edited by Sculley Bradley and Harold W. Blodgett. New York: Norton, 1973.

Wordsworth, William. *Selected Poems and Prefaces.* Edited by Jack Stillinger. Boston: Houghton Mifflin, 1965.

Yeats, W. B. *The Collected Poetry of W. B. Yeats.* New York: Macmillan, 1956.

INDEX

historical consciousness, 4, 19, 32, 33, 37, 43–44, 51, 57, 65, 71, 73, 77, 79, 88–89, 104, 116, 120
Homer: *The Iliad,* 79, 84; *The Odyssey,* 56
"Homestead on the Horsepasture, A," 64
"Honesty," 19, 22, 28
Hopkins, Gerard Manley, 48, 68
Hopper, Edward: *Nighthawks,* 125
humor, 10, 11–13, 15, 24, 28, 31, 83–84, 91, 108–9, 113–14, 120, 121

"Importance of Place, The," 1–2
"In a Dry Time," 31
"In a Springhouse at Night," 39
"In Dismal Gorge," 45
interconnections among Rash's works, 16, 44, 54–55, 66, 104, 123
"In the Solomons," 21
"Into the Gorge," 111–12, 113
"Invocation," 31, 33
irony, 10, 12, 13, 20, 32, 36, 46, 58, 60, 71, 74, 75, 80, 93–94, 95, 102, 108, 116–17, 122

James, William: *The Varieties of Religious Experience,* 70, 132n24
Jocassee Valley/Lake Jocassee, 4, 19–20, 41–44, 48, 57, 59, 64, 65
"Judgment Day," 11, 13
"July, 1949," 33–34
Jung, C. G., 33

Keats, John, 8, 30; "The Eve of St. Agnes," 98, 101
Kephart, Horace, 68, 94; *Our Southern Highlanders,* 82
Korean War, 18, 22, 58, 124

landscape as destiny, 79, 80–81, 102
"Language of Canaan, The," 38–39
"Last Interview," 33
"Last Rite," 15–16, 17, 18, 19, 21, 28, 123
"Last Service," 43
"Last Words," 31

liminality, 14, 36, 58, 67–68
"Lincolnites," 114–15
"Love and Pain," 13, 14
love as theme, 16, 19, 21, 62, 64–65, 70, 80, 85, 91–92, 94, 96, 124
Luther, Martin, 70
Lynyrd Skynyrd, 113–14, 127

Mabinogion, The, 55
"Madison County: 1864," 37, 74
"Madison County: 1934," 105
"Madison County: June, 1999," 47
"Magic Bus, The," 118–19, 134n16
Marion, Jeff Daniel, 3, 29
Marlowe, Christopher: *The Massacre at Paris,* 83
McCarthy, Cormac, 8; *The Road,* 92, 133n15
McCrumb, Sharyn, 60
Melville, Herman: *Moby-Dick,* 72, 84, 87
"Mirror," 51
moral choices as theme, 22, 26, 28, 59, 61, 62, 64–65, 81, 94–95, 108–9
Morgan, Robert, 4, 29, 53, 116
"Morning Service: August, 1959," 40, 69
Muir, Edwin: "One Foot in Eden," 57–58, 65, 79, 102
"Muskellunge," 54–55
"My Father Like a River," 20–21, 22, 23, 54
"My Father's Cadillacs," 10–11
mystery, sense of, 17, 23, 24, 40–41, 49, 51, 79–80, 113, 122–23

nature, attitudes toward, 5, 25, 37, 38–39, 49–54, 68–69, 71, 80, 85–88, 124
Nietzsche, Friedrich, 80, 87
"Night Hawks," 125–26
Night the New Jesus Fell to Earth, The, 3, 7, 8–15, 16, 48, 116, 125
"Night the New Jesus Fell to Earth, The," 11–12
"Notes from Beyond the Pale," 10